"I got distracted while writing [ ]
tracted while reading it, thank g [ ]
both of us! Paying attention is a lost art. If you're ready to master
it, read this!"

Jon Acuff, *New York Times* bestselling author of *Soundtracks*

"Paying attention just may be the most important thing we do as
humans, and we often do such a terrible job at it. Paul Angone's
new book shows us how to fix that; it teaches us how to be more
human. This one is especially overdue."

Jeff Goins, bestselling author of *The In-Between*

"There's a treasure chest filled with gold that's hiding in plain
sight—right under your feet—containing the answers to your
biggest life questions and conundrums. If you are having trouble
finding this treasure, you are not alone. With his signature wit and
wisdom, Paul Angone is back with another beautiful book to help
you dig deeper, dissolve distractions, and listen even more closely
to the clues already guiding you. Spend just a few short hours with
this book, and you will already gain a lifetime of habits to help
you build a more meaningful, fulfilling life."

Jenny Blake, podcaster and author of *Free Time*, *Pivot*,
and *Life After College*

"*Listen to Your Day* is going to help you clean your thinking and
find a peace that you didn't know was possible. Paul Angone ad-
dresses one of the biggest problems of our day. If you have a smartphone in your pocket, you would be smart to read this book again
and again."

Jonathan Pokluda, bestselling author, host of the *Becoming
Something* podcast, and lead pastor of Harris Creek

"Paul is truly a champion for living purposefully and with intention. *Listen to Your Day* provides both deep wisdom and a tangible
road map for tuning out the noise we are all bombarded with and

tuning in to the things that will positively transform your heart—and your life—one day at a time."

"Paul Angone has done it again. *Listen to Your Day* is that rare kind of book that is at once wise, witty, and whimsical. Angone deftly combines insights from psychology and neuroscience, the Bible, and personal experience to help us open our eyes and ears to see and hear the good, the true, and the beautiful in everyday life. He even delivers practical wisdom in a chapter written sitting in a bubble bath. Really! Check out chapter 7. I think this is Paul's best book yet."

"Paul Angone had me at the first paragraph. I don't usually say that a nonfiction book is a page-turner, but this one is just that. Paul is a great writer and thinker. I'm a better person for consuming this content. I highly recommend this book."

LISTEN
TO
YOUR
DAY

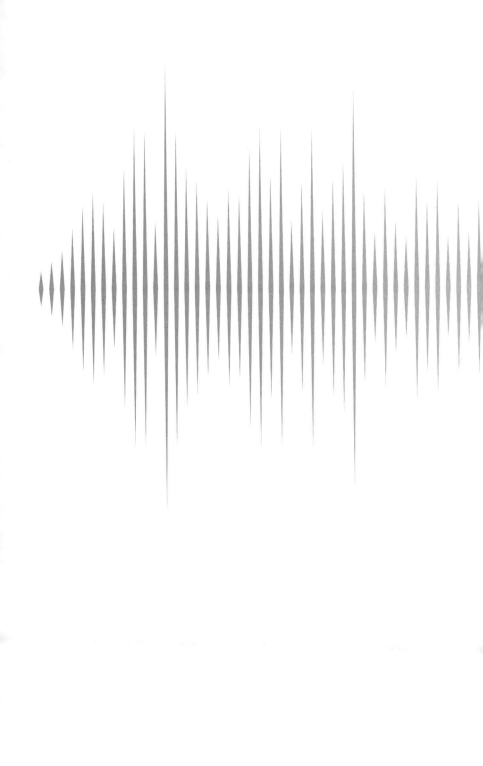

LISTEN
TO
YOUR
DAY

THE LIFE-CHANGING PRACTICE
OF PAYING ATTENTION

PAUL ANGONE

BakerBooks
a division of Baker Publishing Group
Grand Rapids, Michigan

© 2023 by Paul Angone

Published by Baker Books
a division of Baker Publishing Group
PO Box 6287, Grand Rapids, MI 49516-6287
www.bakerbooks.com

Printed in the United States of America

Library of Congress Cataloging-in-Publication Data
Names: Angone, Paul, author.
Title: Listen to your day : the life-changing practice of paying attention / Paul Angone.
Description: Grand Rapids : Baker Books, a division of Baker Publishing Group, [2023] |
    Includes bibliographical references.
Identifiers: LCCN 2022035884 | ISBN 9781540900715 (paperback) | ISBN
    9781540902986 (casebound) | ISBN 9781493437740 (ebook)
Subjects: LCSH: Mindfulness (Psychology) | Attention.
Classification: LCC BF321 .A65 2023 | DDC 158.1/3—dc23/eng/20221007
LC record available at https://lccn.loc.gov/2022035884

The author is represented by The Christopher Ferebee Agency, www. christopherferebee.com.

Baker Publishing Group publications use paper produced from sustainable forestry practices and post-consumer waste whenever possible.

23   24   25   26   27   28   29   7   6   5   4   3   2   1

Contents

To my family.

My wife, Naomi, and our children,
Hannalise, Sierrah, Judah, and Jlynn.
Thank you for all the encouragement and sacrifices
to help make this book happen.
Love you all.

It has become extremely difficult for us to stop, listen, pay attention and receive gracefully what is offered to us.

—Henri Nouwen

Introduction

Seeing through Inattentional Blindness

What would you do if a bear moonwalked right in front of you?
Gasp?
Laugh?
Pull out your phone as quickly as possible to take a video?
What if I told you that you probably wouldn't do any of these things? What if I told you that you most likely wouldn't notice this moonwalking bear at all?

Not because the bear was hidden. It would be right in front of you. And yes, you wouldn't see it.

I know this because over the years, I've seen very smart people from around the world sitting in large classrooms, auditoriums, gyms, and conference halls—managers, VPs, and CEOs from all over the world in a grand ballroom at the Palazzio in Las Vegas—all miss the moonwalking bear that was moving right in front of them. No matter the size, age, education levels, or socioeconomic makeup of the audience, they always miss the moonwalking bear. It's wild. And they can't believe it either.

How is this possible? What am I talking about? Let me explain.

Over the years, I've played the same video in countless keynotes to all kinds of different industries. Maybe you've seen it? (Funny

11

At some level, I think every serious person in psychology has always believed that we don't consciously perceive everything that happens to us. **The shocking thing was that you could show so little is being perceived.**[1]

—Harvard University psychologist Christopher Chabris, PhD, researcher behind inattentional blindness

thing is, I've found that even if people have seen a similar type of video, they still don't notice the moonwalking bear.)

In the video, there are two teams. One in white clothes and the other in black, with one basketball for each team. The narrator asks a simple question: "How many passes does the team in white make?"

The video plays as the audience focuses in, counting the passes. After the passes are completed, the video pauses, and I ask the audience how many passes the team in white made. They all shout out in that excited unison when you're sure you have the right answer, "Thirteen!" They got it right! But then the narrator in the video asks, "But did you see the moonwalking bear?"

"What?!" Gasps and shouts fill the crowd. The video rewinds, and we watch the same sequence. But this time, the audience erupts in laughter as they now see the moonwalking bear that went slowly across the entire screen, which they hadn't seen the first time.

The screen goes black and the narrator says, "It's easy to miss something you're not looking for."[2]

Why does everyone miss the moonwalking bear? It's because they aren't looking for one.

This video is tied into the psychological theory called *inattentional blindness*. A working definition of this phenomenon is "the failure to notice something right in front of you because other attention-demanding tasks are at hand."

I'd argue this definition of inattentional blindness sums up the day-to-day of most of our lives. We miss all the moonwalking bears. We miss the giant revelations, ideas, and truths walking right in front of us because we aren't *actually* looking for them. Or we don't know how to see them even when they pass right in front of us.

But we can shift our attention to start looking for them. We must form the habit and the practice to truly notice the giant truths moonwalking right in front of us.

It's not a problem with our eyesight. It's a problem with our inability to perceive and understand. We are losing the skill and art of paying attention. We think we see, but we don't.

So many of us are crying out for answers to the burning questions in our lives. We're desperate for clarity. So many things feel so ambiguous and confusing.

What path do I take? What job or career do I pursue? Is this the right person for me? What's my calling and passion? How do I parent these kids? If you're from a faith background, you've probably cried out to God more than once to give you the answers.

But maybe God has been answering those prayers for you all along. You just have not seen it. Better put, you have not perceived and understood. We spend most of our days seeing and hearing, yet not paying attention.

Praying for a Miracle

It's like the old parable of the man who is sitting on the roof of his house to escape a rapidly rising flood. He shouts to God to save him.

Studies of visual perception have demonstrated how startlingly little people see when we're not paying attention.[3]
　　　　　　　　　　　　–Siri Carpenter, American Psychological Association

Then a man with a boat comes by and offers the extra space to the man on the roof. "Jump in and I'll get you to safety." The man on the roof refuses. "I know God will save me, so I'll wait here."

Then a firefighter comes by and says to hurry down and he'll get him out of harm's way. The man refuses, saying he is waiting for God to save him.

The water rises higher and a helicopter hovers over him, a voice yelling at him through the megaphone to grab the rope and be pulled to safety. The man refuses and tries yelling up to the helicopter that he's waiting for God to save him.

Well, the water keeps rising and the man on the roof gets swept away.

He goes to heaven and asks God, "Why didn't you save me?"

God responds, "I sent you a boat, a firefighter, and even a helicopter! What more did you want?"

Jesus even warned us about inattentional blindness two thousand years ago:

> You will be ever hearing but never understanding;
>   you will be ever seeing but never perceiving.
> For this people's heart has become calloused;
>   they hardly hear with their ears,
>   and they have closed their eyes.
> Otherwise they might see with their eyes,
>   hear with their ears,
>   understand with their hearts
> and turn, and I will heal them.
>   Matthew 13:14–15 NIV

Having Sight, but Not Seeing

The idea of inattentional blindness goes beyond what we see and hear as well. Famed author and activist Helen Keller was blind and deaf, and yet she *saw* more than most. She understood with her heart and mind. She was paying attention in profound ways that led to wisdom and revelation. Or as Ms. Keller poignantly stated it, "The most pathetic person in the world is someone who has sight, but has no vision."

How do we cultivate the habit and practice of really paying attention? Of seeing, perceiving, and understanding. Of recognizing all the revelation and profound answers we come across every day that we've failed to see as such. Of having sight while also having vision.

> The wise heart will figure out the proper time and proper way to proceed. Yes, there is a time and a way to deal with every situation, even when a person's troubles are on the rise.
>
> Ecclesiastes 8:5–6

Wisdom is knowledge *applied* correctly.

How can we apply knowledge correctly throughout our lives if we are not paying attention?

So the question becomes, how do we properly pay attention to the right things? How do we see and understand? How do we listen to our day, every day, and embark on this simple, yet life-changing, journey?

The goal of this book: **To help you reclaim your own attention and create a lifelong practice of paying attention to things of worth that matter.** Let's get to it.

the most
SUCCESSFUL
and fulfilled
people on this
EARTH ARE SIMPLY
better at paying
ATTENTION TO WHAT'S
important

Paul Angone

ONE

The Epic Journey Right Where You Are

We yearn to go on epic searches for truth and treasure. Just look at popular movies and literature, not just in our day, but in years past. Yet Paolo Coelho, author of the bestselling *The Alchemist*, unmasks such a fallacy:

> A man sets out on a journey, dreaming of a beautiful or magical place, in pursuit of some unknown treasure. At the end of his journey, the man realizes the treasure was with him the entire time.[1]

Like the shepherd boy in his story, we come back from the long, laborious journey where we never found the treasure we were looking for—only to finally see that it was sitting right under us the whole time.

"The grass is always greener on the other side until you get there and realize it's because of all the manure."[2] I wrote that years ago in my book *101 Secrets for Your Twenties*, and I believe it's more true now than ever.

All day we see snapshots of the entire world. Friends experiencing success of all kinds. We see the global green grass and we wonder, "Maybe I would be happier over there. Maybe I'd find my success somewhere else. Maybe *over there* is the answer."

The allure of the unknown treasures "out there" becomes more enticing than simply unearthing the treasure right under us. You have this rich gold mine sitting beneath you, in front of you, all around you. You have treasure waiting for you to discover right where you are!

I think back to a sad story my grandpa would tell me. He grew up on a small farm in Kansas. His mother passed away when he was in his twenties, and all the siblings got together to decide if they would keep the farm or sell it. My grandpa didn't need a second to think about the question—his heart screamed that they should keep it in the family. It was their home.

Yet, an older brother, who everyone knew was a very active alcoholic, adamantly demanded they sell it right away (as he needed to pay off some discreet debts he'd been piling up). I don't know how long the discussion lasted, but in the end my grandpa stepped aside, and the farm was quickly sold for a steal. "Then wouldn't you know it"—my grandpa would always laugh when telling the story, a mixture of heartbreak and justification—"a few years later they'd strike oil on that farm and become rich. And wouldn't you know it, where would they find the oil? Under my mother's garden."

His mom had been digging there her whole life. But she just hadn't dug deep enough.

Your Flavors at Home

For another example, take the documentary series *The Chef's Table*, which follows Michelin-star chefs. Watching these master craftsmen and craftswomen is mesmerizing. But in each one of their stories, I noticed the same pattern: almost the exact same theme emerges every time. The chef would decide to go to France or

I am Massimo Bottura. I close my eyes and I want to understand where I am, cooking is about emotion, it's about culture, it's about love, it's about memory.

—Massimo Bottura, chef patron of Osteria Francescana

some faraway place to learn their techniques. Then they would create some replica version of a restaurant or menu that copied what their mentors taught them.

Then, it would all fail. The chef would burn out, head into the wilderness, and come back home with the realization that *this is where my magic is*. In their own life they would discover their own way. Their signature sauce was simply in unearthing the treasure of flavors from home.

Your Treasure Is Here

What if I told you that you've already been given the answers to your biggest questions? Your day, each day, is speaking to you and showing you so much. It's gold, I'm telling you. The problem is, we don't see it because we're not looking for it.

No, we are focused on the million "attention-demanding tasks" at hand. In today's world, we are filling every pause in our day with a distraction. A literal bear could moonwalk right up to us with a glass of lemonade, just waiting for us to take a picture to get some Instagram content that's ready to go viral, yet we don't see it because our attention is forever elsewhere.

I'm becoming more and more convinced that the most successful entrepreneurs, the most insightful authors, the most hilarious comedians, the most effective teachers and parents are not smarter than the rest of us. **I would argue the most successful and fulfilled people on this earth are simply better at paying attention to what's important**—to the things that matter to them—and then applying those insights to the sphere in which they live.

Paying attention truly is the path to becoming an expert. Experts focus on one thing through a lens that others are not willing to, or cannot, see through. They have simply trained their minds to pay attention to what matters most to them. Then they reveal the truth they see to others who cannot see.

We talk about those rare times when we experience an aha moment. I'd argue we experience these aha moments every day, we just don't recognize them as such.

So this book is not a fad, quick-hit "self-help" book that will change everything for you for about a month until I can sell you another product to change your life for the following month.

No, this book lays out a process that can change your life by changing the way you pay attention to your day, every day. This is a strategic, functional mindfulness to help you stop living an intentionally unintentional life and get the clarity you need and desire.

I will say this many times throughout this book, but we must *pay attention* to the right things. Every day you are making payments through what you're focusing on. The problem is, most of us are making payments with our attention in all the wrong places and not getting enough in return. In this distracted, deafening age, we are dangerously losing the battle for our own attention.

Why are you frustrated? Why are you anxious? Why are you excited? What is your calling? What is your path? The answers lie in the details of your day.

If you are unaware of what is going on all around you, how can you be aware of where you are going?

If you are unaware of the questions that you and your soul are asking, how will you find the answers?

If you are unaware of the time and season you are living in, how will you know if it's time to plant or if it's time to reap?

The Art, Skill, and Practice of Paying Attention

A successful life starts with a humble, curious, and acute awareness.

The Cambridge Dictionary defines *awareness* as "knowledge that something exists, or understanding of a situation or subject at the present time based on information or experience."[3]

Fully living your life begins with an intentional choice to be an active participant in your day—in the magical, the mundane, and the mechanical.

Do not be afraid to pull your head out from under the blankets. I promise you the darkness there is way scarier than the light and the revelation that's all around you.

This book is a call to walk in an awareness that leads to wisdom and revelation.

This is reimagining our lives based on the strategic, important information we are receiving every day.

We've lost the art, skill, and practice of paying attention.

Each day has so much to tell us, if we will only see, hear, and understand. This is a call to pay attention.

We must learn the art, science, and habit of listening to the details of our day and all the answers our day wants to tell us. We must develop a practice and a new lens to view our day through, so that we can recognize the answers right in front of us that we have failed to see.

Reading this book is a great start. The fact that something about this topic caught your eye and you are actively moving toward it says something. It really does. Let's not minimize this first choice.

So this will not just be a theoretical book for you to read. This book is a companion in action. I will be asking you what you see *for yourself*, not just telling you what you should be seeing.

I want to help you uncover your revelation. Your revelation for your unique, amazing life. You have a purpose. You have a name. You have a path. I don't know what that is. But you will. As you pay attention to your day and the steps I lay out, you will see and understand.

And I promise, if you start here, if you begin to form this new habit of listening to your day, you will be amazed at all the breakthrough ideas, creativity, healthier relationships, job satisfaction and growth, insights, personal development, joy, and peace you will experience.

You will no longer feel powerless, like life is just happening to you without your knowledge or control. No, your eyes and ears will be opened in ways you've never experienced before. You'll stop feeling like you're simply an actor or actress in your life. Instead, you'll be the writer, director, producer, and the talent! You'll shift from passive to engaged participant.

By the end of this book, you'll have clarity to your purpose and passion. You'll have new book ideas, business ideas, parenting ideas, and strategies in designing your day based on *your* design. You'll have healthier relationships as you learn to pay attention to those in front of you.

You can't see something you're not looking for. Now, it's time to start looking. Let's spot the moonwalking bears right in front of you. Every day we are given countless gifts of clarity. We must learn the science, art, and practice of seeing them. We need to listen to those moments when the Designer reveals to you his design.

And if you are the praying type, maybe sit and meditate on this right now as I do the same.

"Give me eyes to see. Give me ears to hear. So that I might understand."

PART ONE

The LIFE-CHANGING POWER *of* PAYING ATTENTION

Believe it or not, your whole life is influenced by what you pay attention to.

When you give your time, energy, affection, and money to whatever it is you are focusing on, you are literally *paying* someone or something your attention. Like you are giving them a $20 bill for your engagement. Time is money, and your attention is your currency.

There is a war going on right now, more than ever before, for your attention.

Unfortunately, for many of us it feels like we are dangerously close to losing this war. We don't seem to understand how little we are paying attention, because this day and age has become so advanced in taking our attention from us. And it's happened without us realizing it, because we willingly let it be stolen.

I don't think many of us wake up, throw off the sheets, and say "All right, I'm ready to be manipulated today! I can't wait!" Yet, in reality, this is exactly what's happening.

As Vance Packard wrote in his bestselling book *The Hidden Persuaders*, "Many of us are being influenced and manipulated, far more than we realize, in the patterns of our everyday lives."[1]

Packard wrote his groundbreaking, culture-shaking book about the advertising world and how sophisticated it was becoming in tapping into behavioral psychology to sell us stuff in 1957. Since then, the "hidden persuaders" have become more deeply entrenched and manipulative in the entire technological system for which we live and breathe. The Hidden Persuaders of today's world have become Master Manipulators. What they are striving to obtain from us more than anything? Our *attention*.

We must fight to pay attention. To the right things. To things of worth and meaning. To changing the way we see our day so that we can truly see it for the gift it is.

Comedian Dave Chappelle, in an insightful interview on *CBS This Morning*, described his choice to walk away from "50 million dollars" and fame, quitting the Chappelle Show at the height of its popularity. He explained why he left and detailed his journey toward physical, mental, and emotional health:

> I started resting. I started paying attention to myself. I have actual relationships with my kids. I have been all over the country, touring all my life, but I never *saw* anything. Now, I've *seen everything*. . . . The way I engaged the world was different.[2]

In today's world we are living in the raging winds of hurry and distraction. Deafening noise. Broken windows. Muddy windows. Windows that have been boarded up for so long we no longer realize they are even there. We are constantly being told how we should be looking at the world and what specific portal we should be looking through—all in an attempt to detain our attention from looking anywhere else.

We are currently losing the battle for our own attention, but we cannot lose the war. We must take back where we are *paying* our attention. We must start to intentionally decide where our attention is being placed. Before we can see, we must begin removing the things blocking our sight. Before we can hear *anything*, we must limit some of the noise.

The main question becomes, *Where the heck do we start?*

TWO

The Lure of the Distraction

We are distracting ourselves from our own distractions.

How many of us can't even watch a TV show all the way through without also scrolling through our phones? We have a phone in hand, a laptop on our lap, a TV across the room, and a "smart" watch on our wrist, all competing for our attention, sometimes at the same time. And then not to mention some kids, some family, some friends who are asking for our attention as well.

Our attention is divided, sliced and diced into so many different pieces, that it is barely recognizable. We're left with the bits and pieces while some form of distraction gets the choice meat.

We don't feel like we have a moment to ourselves, yet all the moments we do have, we instantly fill them with a distraction *away* from ourselves.

Maybe we don't want as much time to ourselves as we think we do.

Maybe we believe we want time to think, yet if we took an audit of our daily actions, it would look quite the opposite. Far too often, whenever we have time to ourselves, we distract ourselves from it. Why?

Maybe we're scared of those times to ourselves because we're afraid of what we will hear. We don't want to pay attention because we don't want to grapple with the truths we will see. Or the thoughts we might think. Or the feelings we might feel if we allow ourselves to be still and see. If we can stay busy and distracted enough, then we can have an excuse not to make the changes we may need to make.

Yet, we know distracting ourselves from our fears does nothing to eliminate them. It just hides them deeper in our minds. Allowing them to make their home there instead of facing these fears head-on and throwing them out the door.

Because many of us can feel that we're either kind of spinning around on the same nauseating teacups of life or we're kind of stuck. We know the path we're on is not the one we necessarily want to walk down, yet veering off and exploring feels too overwhelming or frightening to attempt. We don't even know the first step we would take to get to who we want to be.

> Our attention is divided, sliced and diced into so many different pieces, that it is barely recognizable. We're left with the bits and pieces while some form of distraction gets the choice meat.

So how do we pay attention to the important details of our day if we are willingly, yet unintentionally, distracting ourselves from seeing and hearing? **We are so busy, yet we rarely feel like we're getting much done. Are we busy in the *right* places?**

Could someone figure out what you think is most important to you in life by what you spend the most time intentionally paying attention to in a day? If not, why? Seems like a contradiction is running the show then. Either your thought process is lying to you, or your actions are.

I would *not* tell you right now that my phone is the most important thing in my life. Yet, my actions and time spent do not back up that statement. I am daily living a contradiction, and that does not feel like a wise way to live healthy and whole.

Digital Junk Food

There's so much noise—unrelenting amounts of *stuff* that we are constantly digesting through our phones, watches, and social media feeds. It's like eating a bowl of M&Ms with chocolate milk for breakfast. If you've stuffed yourself full of junk food, you don't start craving a bowl full of steamed broccoli for dessert.

Same goes for our attention. The more we focus on junk, the harder it is to concentrate on things of depth and importance. It's becoming extremely difficult to think long and hard about *anything*. Let's say, for example, we start trying to solve a problem in our minds. We hit a difficult spot, a snag, in our thinking, then we quickly escape from the thought into something, anything. Before we realize it, we're in the spinning vortex of noise—TV, blaring music, or all the *internetness*. It's become a reflex. A pain tolerance of sorts.

We have too many easily accessible escape hatches from the hard work of thinking through something important. There's a tipping point to paying attention. But too many of us stop before we get to the heart of what we need to see and understand.

We are addicted to the quick hit of a distraction. Like marathon runners who train themselves to push through discomfort, we have to train ourselves to push through the urge of distraction.

In fact, while writing these last two paragraphs I scrolled over to the internet browser behind this document numerous times. Only when I started clicking on random tabs did I stop myself and think, *Why am I doing this? What am I looking for? Get back to work!*

By constantly filling ourselves with more and more instant information and entertainment, we end up distracting ourselves from the solutions we really need.

Do we actually want the answers? I think most of us would say we want answers about the important questions we've been asking about our lives. But do our actions back up this belief? Well . . . Distraction is simply letting fear and anxiety win.

A Culture of Escape Artists

We've become a culture of escape artists. Magicians of sorts. Disappearing in plain sight. We're not pulling a cape over ourselves and teleporting to another room. No, we're escaping into our screens. We don't want to tackle the problem in front of us, so we run and hide in infinite scrolling. Yet, through this act of continual escape, we end up avoiding the most important parts of our life.

In my previous book *25 Lies Twentysomethings Need to Stop Believing*, I referred to this problem as our Obsessive *Connection* Disorder—"The need to constantly be connected [through some device], which in turn leaves us incredibly disconnected."[1]

We check the phone not as much for entertainment as for escape. A numbing of sorts. A distraction from the distraction of all the distractions. And, most times, we don't choose to do it. We don't even want to do it. We are compelled to do it. Our fingers start scratching before we realize we have an itch. . . . Like smoking another cigarette, we swear we will stop and get it under control. *But just after this next one.*[2]

This goes hand in hand with what I first defined in my book *101 Secrets for Your Twenties* as our Obsessive *Comparison* Disorder— "Our compulsion to constantly compare ourselves with others, producing unwanted thoughts and feelings that drive us to depression, consumption, anxiety, and all-around joyous discontent."[3]

I don't define this as such to make light of those with obsessive-compulsive disorder. I do this to talk about the serious addiction so many of us are quietly battling in our constant need to be

WE ARE SO BUSY, YET WE RARELY FEEL LIKE WE'RE GETTING MUCH DONE. ARE WE BUSY IN THE RIGHT PLACES? —PAUL ANGONE

connected. Then on social media this addiction of connection quickly turns into the warts of comparison. Connect, compare, connect, compare, read a new headline that fills us with anxiety and fear, connect, compare, connect, compare.

Would you down pink cotton candy and then keep riding on the swinging chairs at the carnival, even though it's making you sicker and sicker? No, you'd get off. So why do we keep jumping into this cycle of obsessively connecting and comparing? Why do we keep spinning around in circles feeling sicker instead of continuing forward on the journey we know we're supposed to embark on?

We need to analyze these distractions and begin escaping them if we are going to become able to pay attention to what matters most.

THREE

Un-Dividing Our Divided Attention

If you took English in high school, you probably embarked on a personal odyssey to make it through the 12,109 lines of Homeric hexameter that is *The Odyssey*.

In the epic, the hero Odysseus embarks on a journey to make it back home after war. While sailing home with his crew, Odysseus is warned by the goddess Circe about the Sirens—beautiful women with songs so alluring that they lead men straight to them. Only when it's too late does their prey realize these "beautiful women" are actually monsters and anyone who hears their song and comes to them will die.

Yet, even with the warning, Odysseus still wants to hear the Sirens' song. He has his men block their ears with beeswax given to them by Circe, and they tie Odysseus to the mast of the ship. Then Odysseus hears the Sirens' song:

> Odysseus, bravest of heroes,
> Draw near to us, on our green island,

Odysseus, we'll teach you wisdom,
We'll give you love, sweeter than honey.
The songs we sing, soothe away sorrow,
And in our arms, you will be happy.
Odysseus, bravest of heroes,
The songs we sing, will bring you peace.

Odysseus is captivated. So much so that he tries to free himself from the ropes tying him down and, in his desperation, he cuts his arms and back. Yet his crew, ears blocked with beeswax, can see the Sirens clearly as the monsters with vicious, crooked claws that they are.

It's interesting that the Sirens' "value proposition"—their promise to anyone who will pay attention to them—is to lure travelers by promising first that they will teach them wisdom. Then they offer love sweeter than honey. They will soothe away sorrow. In their arms, you will be happy and at peace on their lush, green island.

They offer wisdom, love, happiness free from sorrow, and peace on a tropical island. This sounds like the promises of a properly run Instagram account.

Yet, when someone is lured over to the Sirens by these false promises, it leads to their death.

There are different interpretations as to how the men who are lured to them die. "Some believe that the Sirens are cannibals who consume the sailors that they lure over. Others believe that the Sirens are unable to provide food to their visitors, which eventually leads to starvation, as the visitors can't leave because of the Sirens' song."[1]

There is promise of substance, yet none exists. The victims end up dying from their own starvation because they are unable to leave the Sirens' call.

While this image might seem extreme, I do believe this metaphor has piercing comparisons to today's siren call of our smartphones and devices. They call out to us, promising wisdom, peace, love, and happiness that is free from sorrow. Yet, the end result for most of us is more starvation than sustenance.

We don't want to be drawn into our phones for hours and hours a day, yet we feel incapable of stopping ourselves. We become heavy tech users. "User," of course, being the same name we give to someone who hits up their iPhones and someone who takes a hit of a drug. Interesting.

Both the drug and the phone end up using us more than we do them. And like the Sirens' call, they captivate and capture us for their own devious devices.

Think I am being melodramatic? The hundreds of thousands of extremely intelligent people who have created apps and social media platforms with one goal in mind—to be as addictive as possible—might argue otherwise.

In a BBC interview, former technology engineer for Mozilla and Jawbone employee Aza Raskin stated:

> It's as if they're taking behavioral cocaine and just sprinkling it all over your interface and that's the thing that keeps you, like, coming back and back and back.[2]

Behavioral cocaine is a fairly strong word choice from an insider engineer, isn't it?

Raskin had more to add:

> Behind every screen on your phone, there are generally, like, literally a thousand engineers that have worked on this thing to try to make it maximally addicting.[3]

Facebook's own internal investigations that were leaked in 2021 from whistleblower Frances Haugen show that the company itself knew that one out of eight[4] Facebook users showed "problematic use"[5] as to the amount of time they were spending on Facebook and how it was interfering with their daily lives.

And I'm sure Facebook's internal investigations have a little different threshold for what is "problematic use" (what us regular people might label as "addiction") than a parent of a child might.

And in no ironic twist of human language, Mark Zuckerberg's recent creation Meta, with its 3D immersive world, is the latest invention we need to give all our attention and time (and therefore money) to. Do you know what "Meta" means in Hebrew? Dead. In both present and past tenses. Interesting. Meta is more *meta* than we even realized.

I think one conclusion is fairly clear—social media platforms and apps are rarely created for purely altruistic reasons to help humankind. Even if their intentions were "noble" at the beginning.

Whether it's in the first meeting between founders or the first meeting with stakeholders, the main goal of each platform and app is to increase the number of users and the amount of time you spend on it.

Basically, each app and social media platform knows how distracted we are, so they need to create the most engaging (and addictive) platform they can to get your undivided attention. Or at least a third of your attention along with the two other things you are dividing your attention between.

Social media platforms such as Facebook, Snapchat, and Instagram produce the same neural circuitry that is caused by gambling and recreational drugs to keep consumers using their products as much as possible. Studies have shown that the constant stream of retweets, likes, and shares from these sites cause the brain's reward area to trigger the same kind of chemical reaction seen with drugs like cocaine. In fact, neuroscientists have compared social media interaction to a syringe of dopamine being injected straight into the system.[6]

—Jena Hilliard, The Addiction Center

A Carefully Constructed System of . . . Con Artists?

Social critic and bestselling author Vance Packard tried valiantly to *persuade* us to be aware of the "depth manipulators" and how we are letting them invade the privacy of our minds. And this was in the year of our Lord 1957!

How much more serious and alarming is Packard's prophetic warning now.

What advertisers were doing in the 1950s is like a child making a Play-Doh pancake, thinking you'll be tricked into eating it. Compare that to what technology is feeding us now.

The hidden persuaders of today's age are not brazen, vulgar *Mad Men*. The hidden persuaders of today, and overwhelmingly tomorrow, are much more hidden. So hidden that we are not consciously aware of what they are doing to us. They are what people in the sixties feared subliminal messages were, except this time, all-encompassing and intrusive—artificial intelligence (AI) and algorithms solely constructed to understand everything about you so that you can become a "user." So that you can be captured, manipulated, and exploited based off information you have freely given.

These social media platforms gain your confidence and trust so that you will give it more than you realize. Really, isn't that the definition of an effective con artist? A good con artist simply shows you what you *want* to see and nothing more.

Search engines and social media platforms, a law unto themselves, are the con artists of today.

> The most serious offense many of the depth manipulators commit, it seems to me, is that they try to invade the privacy of our minds. It is this right to privacy in our minds—privacy to be either rational or irrational—that I believe we must strive to protect.
> —Vance Packard, *Hidden Persuaders*

WE USED TO ANSWER THE PHONE ONLY WHEN IT WAS RINGING.

NOW OUR PHONE IS CALLING TO US EVEN WHEN IT DOESN'T MAKE A SOUND.

These search engines, social media platforms, and you know, your Alexa or Google Nest that is in your living room and designed to hear you, are all doing just that. Listening very carefully and very well.

Search results are tailored to what the search engine knows you want to see.

Have you ever gone on the interweb and all of a sudden you start seeing the same ad pop up on all the different sites you are visiting? *What a coincidence*, you might even think. *I was just looking to buy something on that site.*

Of course many of us realize now that this is no coincidence but a marketing strategy called retargeting, a technology that puts a cookie in your browser once you're on their site so that they can follow you around the internet and serve you ads wherever you wander to.

Isn't this the definition of a stalker?

Our twenty-first-century sophisticated stalker that keeps showing up wherever we go. Shouldn't we be more alarmed than we are?

Or as Marie Konnkovia quoted in her book *The Confidence Game* from famed con artist Frank Abagnale Jr., who was well-documented in the movie *Catch Me If You Can*,

> What I did fifty years ago as a teenage boy is four thousand times easier to do today because of technology. Technology breeds crime. It always has, and always will.[7]

Every TV show, YouTube channel, podcast, social media platform, news broadcast, social media influencer—they all strategically want one thing: your attention.

A con artist isn't a good speaker. A con artist is a good listener.
—Marie Konnkovia, psychologist and author of *The Biggest Bluff*

Again, your attention is currency. They do not want you to leave. When you pay them your attention, you are paying them. They will do whatever is in their power to keep it, some with rapidly adapting algorithms, studying your every move, AI informing their quest to keep your attention for as long as humanly possible.

Now tell me, how is this so different than the Sirens in *The Odyssey*—capturing your attention at any price, offering you life to the fullest, but in the end it lacks substance and leads to the starvation of your soul? That, or just instantly being consumed by it. Neither sounds very life-giving to me.

In her article "Why It's Good to Be Bored," Elle Hunt writes, "It takes time and attention to scroll through Instagram or play Candy Crush, but at the end of it, you're not satisfied, because you didn't do the harder work of figuring out: 'What do I really want to do?' It's a vicious cycle: you got some engagement, but it wasn't the thing you needed."[8]

The Selfie Movement

Google reports that its Android devices take 93 million selfies per day, and in one poll, eighteen-to-twenty-four-year-olds reported that every third photo they take is a selfie.[9] Some subjects in one study reported taking more than eight selfies a day. For many of us, snapping and then posting selfies has become a way of life.

A study of 113 undergrad women in Canada aimed to better understand the effects on anxiety and body image when posting a selfie. The study consisted of first a control group that read a travel brochure, then a second group who could take only one picture of themselves and post it unfiltered on Instagram or Facebook. Then the third group who could take multiple pictures of themselves and use filtering apps to make them look better before they posted.

The results? They were different than maybe you'd think. First, the control group who just read a travel brochure and didn't take a single pic of themselves, yes, they felt the best about their lives. Maybe no surprise there.

But the two other groups—that just took one picture and posted versus the other who took many pictures and filtered and posted them—both experienced similar levels of anxiety and felt less physically attractive.[10] But the group who could retake and retouch did not lose as much confidence as the group who could take only one photo.

Now an older generation might look at the selfie-taking young and conclude they're all a bunch of narcissists. But Narcissus in Greek mythology fell in love with his own reflection. The evidence doesn't seem to support that assessment.

What I see with our addiction to posting selfies is not narcissism but an insatiable desire for validation and a yearning to be seen.

> What I see with our addiction to posting selfies is not narcissism but an insatiable desire for validation and a yearning to be seen.

In a culture of completely divided attention, we are desperately crying out for anyone to pay attention to us for any reason, whether it means I wear little clothing or I try to jump from a bridge onto a small wooden post a hundred feet off the ground.

We post our cry for attention, our cry to be seen, then we anxiously and irrationally check the stats within minutes and throughout the day to see how many likes, hearts, and validations we've received.

Then, in another twist of irony, if we aren't seen enough for our liking, we quickly delete the post just in case anyone is actually taking notice.

But the problem we all know too well is that the validation is never enough.

40

What Do We Do with All This Tech?

Now I'm not saying we should do away with iPhones and go back to those sexy pagers rocking our hips like we were all ER doctors waiting to be called into surgery. All I'm asking is, should we be answering the call of our phones so many times? Or answering the song of the Sirens these distractions promise us?

We used to answer the phone only when it was ringing. Now our phone is calling to us even when it doesn't make a sound.

Is all this time spent on the phone, or whatever device, helping you pay attention to the really important things of your life? Knowing the latest headlines of today's news cycle, what does that do for your day? For your mind? For your mental and emotional state? What does scrolling through highlight reels of fifty people on social media do for your day?

> What you pay attention to the most should be what you care about the most, shouldn't it?

Is all this time spent, with the average person touching their smartphone over 2,600 times a day,[11] helping you pay attention to the important details of your day, or is it a distraction away from it?

What you pay attention to the most should be what you care about the most, shouldn't it?

What you direct your attention to the most throughout the day is what you're telling the world, your mind, and your soul that you care about the most.

If you start the day with your phone and end the day with your phone, what do you think that says about the importance of the phone in your life?

If they are being honest, what do your spouse, kids, or parents think is the most important thing in your life?

Something to think about as we move on. I don't ask these questions to guilt or shame. I ask them because I want us to truly be honest about what we are paying the most attention to each day. Because if it feels like you don't have enough clarity or answers in your life, maybe it's because you're paying your attention in all the wrong places.

So as we begin our quest of paying attention to what our day is telling us, to seeking wisdom and truth that is life-giving and speaks directly to the heart of the way we were designed, maybe we need to take a lesson from the sailors who saved Odysseus's life and shove some metaphorical beeswax in our ears.

Or like a horse that has an important journey in front of them and their owner does not want them to be scared or distracted by everything around them, maybe we need to put blinders on so that we can focus directly ahead at the goals in front of us.

Putting This into Practice

If we want to listen to our day and what it is telling us, then we need to form some new daily habits. The first one is to limit the distractions and noise that are blocking our eyes and ears.

As we grow up, we learn about the importance of impulse control. We learn to (sometimes) stop ourselves from spending money we don't have on stuff we don't need. We stop ourselves from yelling at the customer, classmate, or colleague who is making us angry, and we learn to calmly ask them a question instead. We stop the impulse to punch our neighbor in the face for continually letting their dog poop on our front lawn. We know that drinking alcohol at one o'clock on a Wednesday afternoon is not going to help the rest of the day go well, so we resist.

Yet with all these ways we actively engage our impulse control, we seem completely powerless or unaware or maybe we just don't even care to fight the rapid, ongoing, every-hour impulse to jump on our phone, social media, or the internet without thinking.

Tech engineers like Aza Raskin, who helped design "the infinite scroll" so that you can endlessly scroll without ever clicking, know the struggle you are having with this impulse, and many are exploiting it. As Raskin explained: "If you don't give your brain time to catch up with your impulses, you just keep scrolling."[12]

So first off, we need to start practicing new habits. And a simple, small one that I want you to work on today, right now, is catching yourself before following the unconscious urge.

We must start formulating the practice of being conscious of what we are doing unconsciously. What do I mean?

I'm not trying to be a Luddite alarmist arguing that we need to do away with all new technologies. What I am arguing for, right now, is for you to choose how you're using these technologies. And start thinking about how they are using you. Intentionally choose to go on them or not.

Your mind, your family, your whole well-being truly depends on this. Don't be manipulated in your depths. Or, put more starkly, don't let social media and the internet, and all that it's become, contaminate your well! How can you expect to draw water from a well that you continually allow to be tainted?

I ask you to consciously catch yourself and pause before jumping on your phone, computer, or internet browser.

I want you to be intentional about not mindlessly jumping on some device when you feel those awkward, uncomfortable, boring gaps in your day.

Don't fill those gaps with instant junk. It's like we're chain-smoking our phones, lighting up and getting a hit before we even realize what we're doing.

Catch yourself. Stop yourself. Then simply get up, put down the phone, and do something else.

Take a five-minute walk. Prepare a healthy snack. Clean something. Pray. Lie down on the ground and put your feet on a chair. I'm serious. When I was studying for finals in college and I'd hit a block, this would be my go-to position to help revive myself and launch new thoughts.

Then I want you to write down the thoughts that come to your mind. Don't edit them. They don't have to be profound or life-changing. Heck, maybe they will be! Or maybe you won't realize how profound they are until you revisit them later.

I just want us to begin to reprogram our habit of filling gaps in our day with noise and distraction. Instead, I want us to begin forming the new habit of intentionally stopping and thinking about what we *want and need* to fill those gaps with. Of being open to new thoughts and ideas. I want us to fill those gaps by listening to the underlying music of our day.

Obviously this habit is not going to be obtained in a day, but can you make a goal with me right now to form a new habit?

As James Clear writes in *Atomic Habits*:

All big things come from small beginnings. The seed of every habit is a single, tiny decision. But as that decision is repeated, a habit sprouts and grows stronger. Roots entrench themselves and branches grow. The task of breaking a bad habit is like uprooting a powerful oak within us. And the task of building a good habit is like cultivating a delicate flower one day at a time.[13]

Let's choose to stop running to distraction, and see where that takes us.

GOAL:

Write down that goal in your own words of making an intentional choice and forming a new habit of not allowing yourself to have the Phone Reflex. What's one action you can begin to take today to limit the endless distractions?

THOUGHTS:

When you feel boredom creeping in or you feel awkward, instead of instantly jumping on your phone, stop and think about what else at that moment you can pay attention to. Write down what you saw, heard, thought, or noticed in these moments.

FOUR

Paying Attention to How You Pay Attention

Before I stepped out on my own to be a full-time author and speaker, I was a marketing specialist for a large university with multiple campuses and an online program.

It was a busy job. A stressful job. (Professors with PhDs don't always appreciate you telling them how they should "sell" their academic program.) And a fun job getting to work with a wonderful, creative, supportive team, with three of us sharing separate corners of one office.

Believe you me, marketing and advertising professionals are experts at directing attention. Because that's their job. And my bosses David, Rafi, Brent, and creative director Christian were really good at what they did.

It was there that I first started learning about "inattentional blindness" through the vice president of marketing, David Peck. He would show the "moonwalking bear" video to a roomful of the smartest people you'll ever have in one space. He was trying to make an important point to them about branding and marketing, but also I think he really just enjoyed getting to trick PhDs who missed seeing the bear, which they always did.

Then Rafi would talk about the phenomenon and psychology of buying a car. He would explain how most people don't really notice the brands and styles of cars around them as they drive throughout the day. That is, until they pick the car they really want to buy, or they buy one. Now they can't believe the coincidence that they see the same make and model everywhere. It's like it's following them.

But in actuality, nothing really changed. There wasn't some timely uptick in sales just because they bought that car too. No, they are now *seeing* the cars that have always been there. Now they are looking for them. They are aware.

Seeing the Toilet at the Restaurant Table

I've experienced this recently, because the last few years my family has gotten into acting in commercials. Long story—with many side stories in between—but we've been able to have some really fun adventures all around the country as a family because of it.

For instance, my wife Naomi, our four kids, and I went to Malibu, California, to be in a VRBO billboard print shoot. They dressed us in tuxes and luxurious dresses, and we took photos in front of a Malibu mansion like we had rented this place out for the family reunion of a lifetime.

Then later that month I was back in LA with my daughter Sierrah for a TV commercial. When the day of filming came about, we found ourselves sitting in an abandoned Macaroni Grill that was filled with about fifty crew members and twenty "extras" who all made the abandoned restaurant look like a pleasant space to eat.

At our table was me, my real daughter, a fake son, and a fake wife, whose chair at the dinner table was a toilet. Yes, she sat next to us at the dinner table on a toilet. We then filmed the same scene, all day, from countless angles and with various expressions, of my fake wife feeling the pains of an oncoming emergency bathroom visit. And her frantically rushing to find the nearest bathroom. (Thankfully the toilet she was sitting on was being used only as a metaphor.)

Why do I bring up these stories? Since I've been home, I've noticed every VRBO ad and have recognized many sidebar ads for VRBO popping up on different websites. One, because I was just in a VRBO ad, so I'm looking for them. And two, through the magical technology of retargeting, if you visit a company's website, those ads are now going to be following you around the interweb through tracking.

I have also intently watched every pharmaceutical ad that's come on TV. I'm not in them, but now I'm *really* seeing them. I'm paying attention to the silly and mundane things they are having the actors do in the background while the narrator reads off all the terrible things that could happen to you if you take the medication.

Because again, I experienced being in one firsthand, so now I'm watching them through the lens of personal experience. I'm seeing what my eyes have been opened to see. Now, if you see a pharmaceutical commercial featuring a lady on a toilet, you can look for me in the restaurant scene as I show proper concern for my fictitious wife when she frantically rushes to the bathroom.

Seeing the Truth around You

Or even better, think right now about how wild it is that so many people are constantly on their phones. Visualize it. Now go look for it.

If you're a student, walk around your campus and start counting. At your office, at your next meeting, count how many times coworkers try to pull off the "I'm looking at my phone under the table and I think no one notices what I'm doing." Which usually most people don't see, because they are on their phone as well. But if you focus your attention on how many people are on their phones in a given situation, you will now notice it.

Some people call it "manifesting" thoughts into real life, but I would argue that it's turning your *attention* to some specific thing by turning your *thoughts* to what is already there or to the opportunities for it to be there. You see what you're looking for.

The Rule of 7

Marketers and advertisers know this challenge all too well, which is why the "Marketing Rule of 7" came to fruition. This concept comes from all the way back in the 1930s and is still utilized today. Basically, advertisers figured out that you need to see a product image or a message about seven times before you'll even recognize that you're seeing it.

Now, however, I believe that number is higher. We are so saturated with images, advertisements, and messages that today we most likely need to see something many more times before we even recognize it is there. But once we really see it, we start looking for it and might take action on it.

This is also the power and the peril of confirmation bias. We see only the info we want to see.

For an example of the peril of "seeing only what we want to see," watch the documentary *Made You Look*. This documentary is about the true story of trusted, respected art dealer Ann Friedman, who worked for Knoedler & Company that was founded in 1846. She unknowingly (or at least without sufficient proof that it was "knowingly") sold counterfeit paintings from some of the most famous Abstract Expressionists like Jackson Pollock and Mark Rothko. Ms. Friedman sold over eighty million dollars of these paintings for over a decade, overlooking any evidence every step of the way that might prove that the paintings were fakes, because she knew "the truth."

Also we see confirmation bias played out to extreme levels in the current political landscape. Both sides yelling at each other because each side believes that they know the full truth and that those on other side are complete idiots.

So why am I bringing up all this advertising and marketing information in a non-marketing-and-advertising book? Why am I talking about the peril of confirmation bias? What does any of this have to do with listening to your day and paying attention?

Well, the lesson of *we see what we're looking for* is a profound one.

What if we applied these principles not to our marketing strategies but to the way we live and see our day, every day. How can we use this strategy to combat inattentional blindness and truly see what is in front of us?

What if we applied the same principle of we see what we're looking for and combine it with this Bible verse from the apostle Paul, teaching the people of Philippi:

> Finally, brothers and sisters, whatever is true, whatever is noble, whatever is right, whatever is pure, whatever is lovely, whatever is admirable—if anything is excellent or praiseworthy—think about such things.
>
> Philippians 4:8 NIV

I don't think Paul was teaching people to think about what is noble, lovely, pure, excellent, and praiseworthy so that they could naively trick themselves into having better thoughts.

No, I believe he was admonishing them to think about these amazing aspects of life so they could *see* how rich their lives were with these things.

You see what you're looking for.

If you're thinking about Ford trucks, you're going to pay attention to and see Ford trucks.

If you were in a pharmaceutical commercial sitting next to your fake wife on a toilet, you're going to pay attention to and

we will see
what we are
looking for

— paul angone

Designed by Elizabeth Tenyer
for *Listen to Your Day:*
The Life-Changing Practice of Paying Attention

see pharmaceutical commercials and the silly things the actors are having to do.

If you wake up and start thinking about all the ways you are blessed, you are going to see and pay attention to all the ways you are blessed.

If you wake up, look at your Instagram post from the night before, and see that it didn't get as many likes as you thought it should, you're going to go through the day seeing ways you're unliked.

If you wake up and think about how great your kids are, you're going to recognize proof for how great they are.

Really, it's just a simple principle of perspective. The artist who stares at the flower from behind is going to draw a very different portrait than the artist who is studying the flower from the front.

If you look at your spouse through the lens of all the ways they are falling short in meeting "your" happiness, then they are going to continually not meet your expectations.

We start radically changing the way we listen to each day and what we pay attention to so that we can experience more peace, clarity, and joy. It's an amazing way to live.

As philosophy professor and author Dallas Willard poignantly described, "The ultimate freedom we have as human beings is the power to select what we will allow or require our minds to dwell upon."[1]

Paying attention is a choice—a very important one that we're failing to recognize as such. We are not powerlessly overrun by distractions. Our minds do not have to be fixated on what brings us anxiety and despair. We can intentionally pay attention and see the good, the worthy, and the life-giving in every day.

We are no longer unintentionally blind to this choice. It is now ours to make. Like the movie *Indiana Jones and the Last Crusade*, where Indiana is met with the life-or-death choice of what grail to drink from—to drink from the gold and flashy that brings death or the everyday cup that brings eternal life. It is imperative for our body and soul that we also "choose wisely."

Moving forward in the following chapters, we're going to analyze different ways of paying attention and mindset models to clarify our focus and encourage us to pay attention differently to what matters most.

PERSPECTIVE PRACTICE:

First, think about a piece of clothing you really want to buy or a car you'd love to drive. Close your eyes right now and visualize it in your mind. Then, as you go about your day, I want you to count how many times you see that piece of clothing or car.

The next day, I want you to think about how blessed you are. Think about all the good things in your life and write them down. Then throughout the day, keep that mindset and begin writing down all the blessings you missed initially. Once you start paying attention to them, you'll see so many more.

FIVE

The Importance of Awkward, Boring, and Quiet Spaces

When was the last time you experienced significant and purposeful silence? Was it right after you woke up? Was it while you were in your car running errands? Or can you not remember? Does the thought of silence fill you with dread? Or do you find it . . . boring?

Many of us attempt to remove awkwardness and boredom from our day. But we shouldn't fill every second of our waking hours with noise. And as numerous studies have shown, allowing ourselves to be bored can help lead to creativity, self-awareness, and better mental health.

Here's a paradox of our current culture. We celebrate authenticity and awkwardness in others. We don't want our role models, politicians, pastors, actors, professors to look and sound the same as they always have.

That's wonderful. I'm all for it.

Yet, we personally don't want to feel awkward. I'd argue the paradox of our culture is that we have undertaken an all-out war against awkward in our day. The death of awkward. Meaning we have removed any awkward space and pauses throughout the day. Anytime we remotely feel awkward, we escape. We quickly avoid that awkward space and fill it with our phones or some form of entertainment.

Yet, we are missing so much by removing boredom and awkward moments throughout our day. I'll expound on this later in the book, but just know that our minds desperately need silence, awkwardness, and boredom.

> We can't let our days become an unending, unceasing cacophony of noise. If we do, how will we hear anything? It's like music. A great song can't actually be a song without the silent pauses in between the notes.

We can't let our days become an unending, unceasing cacophony of noise. If we do, how will we hear anything? It's like music. A great song can't actually be a song without the silent pauses in between the notes.

Psychotherapist and a Fellow of the American Institute of Stress Bryan Robinson discusses the need for boredom:

> It's critical for brain health to let yourself be bored. . . . Social neuroscientists have found that the brain has a default network mode that is on when we're disengaged from doing. Boredom can actually foster creative ideas, refilling your dwindling reservoir, replenishing your work mojo and providing an incubation period for embryonic work ideas to hatch.[1]

Yet, we are frantically filling our minds with more, no matter what it is. Something. Anything. Just don't let me sit here and think.

We are constantly filling these gaps in our days with more, which in turn is constantly giving us less. We're actually draining our mental "reservoir" when we won't stop adding to it. The more anxious, awkward, and alone we feel, the more prone we are to jump on our phone. Being on our phone is more likely to lead us to feeling more anxious and alone, which heightens the struggle instead of alleviating it.

As I wrote in *101 Questions You Need to Ask in Your Twenties*, "When we remove all awkward, we remove all possibilities for unexpected amazing."[2]

We discussed in previous chapters how we're prone to fill all our open spaces throughout the day with stuff and distractions. Not only are we filling our thoughts up with whatever spills onto our screen, but we're also missing all the things we could and should be paying attention to throughout our day.

If we're going to listen to our day, then there have to be times when we're not physically listening to anything else. I've recently been going on the same hike day after day, and I can't help but notice how many people I pass who have some kind of earbuds in their ears. If they are hiking by themselves, around eight out of ten people I pass are listening to something. We're all going to great lengths to be here, in this quiet, open space, and yet we can't help ourselves from filling our ears and mind with something other than our own thoughts.

If you do happen to pass me on that trail, I'm not consuming noise, I'm making it. As I'm moving forward, my synapses start firing, and I become engulfed with some idea or message that I want to discuss. If you look at my Instagram Reels (if that's still a thing by the time you're reading this book), you'll see video after video I've made while hiking those hills. I'm coming up with ideas instead of consuming a podcast of someone else's.

If we're going to pay attention to the details of our day, then our eyes need to be open to what's happening around us and in us. We need to be aware of what we're paying attention to in the moments where it feels like "nothing" is going on.

Thoughts from the Bathtub

I also wrote some of this book while in the bathtub. Call it an exercise in practicing the art of paying attention that I'll write further about in this book. Also, what can I say, I'm a sucker for a lavender bubble bath. Actually, and this might be too much information, I'm writing this in the bathtub right now.

Winston Churchill dictated some of his most famous speeches from the bathtub or while lying in bed.

Award-winning and esteemed screenwriter Dalton Trumbo, who was infamously exiled for communist ties during the McCarthy hearings, helped write classics like *Roman Holiday*, *Exodus*, *Spartacus*, and *Thirty Seconds Over Tokyo*. His favorite spot to write was the bathtub. So much so, if you venture to his hometown of Grand Junction, Colorado, you can spot a statue of a "bronze antique bathtub with a naked sixty-two-year-old man lounging with coffee at the ready and cigarette in hand while working on a script."[3]

Gwen Stefani, during the aftermath of a very public divorce from her first husband, Gavin Rosedale, talked about the refuge of her bathtub. Stefani went on Ryan Seacrest's radio show and talked about continually taking baths and praying.

Why did Churchill, Trumbo, and Stefani go to the bathtub in those moments when they needed clarity the most? What is it about that space that is special? Or when we take a walk, hike, or while gardening? Even when we're quietly driving in the car or simply doing the dishes? What's the power of these quiet spaces in paying attention to the things that matter most? Are we losing these spaces and their powers?

I feel that Trumbo/Churchill/Stefani energy in the bathtub. When I write in the bathtub, it almost feels like I'm cheating. I'm not sitting at a computer trying to force a thought. When I'm in the bathtub, it's like I'm simply joining in an ongoing conversation. I'm tapping into a flow of thoughts and I'm simply taking notes.

It's like an athlete talking about being in the "zone" where they are not thinking about their stance as they step into the batter's box or the placement of their elbow when they're taking their shot at the hoop. No, all the practice and preparation has made their body movements something they don't have to pay attention to. They aren't thinking about their body at all. They're simply stepping into a flow state, a focused zone where the speed of the game slows down, the basket looks bigger, the ball comes in slower, and they just flow.

Yet, in the bath right now, it's taken me much longer to have any kind of coherent thoughts. I think I know why. Before I hopped into the bath, I was scrolling through social media. It's taken me much longer to cut through the mental haze. It almost feels like I'm tipsy, my mind not able to focus or flow as easily as it has before. I found myself thinking through more superficial things that I'd just seen on my screen.

So the power of my quiet place in paying attention to deeper thoughts and ideas was superseded by what I was paying attention to before I stepped in. I thought I was "mindlessly" viewing social media, and yet my mind was now wrestling with things I'd seen there.

It's like going for a walk to clear your thoughts before an important phone call you need to make to a client. You planned that you'd take a walk to formulate your thoughts and strategy as you try to close a much-needed deal. Yet, before you stepped out the door, you got into a slight argument with your spouse. Of course, right? The stress you were feeling leading up to this call probably didn't help the tone of your voice when you responded to your spouse's request to _____.

Now, on your walk, you're trying to think about your call in five minutes but instead you're forming responses to everything your spouse just said as you replay the argument. The quiet space is not quiet in your mind. You jump on the call frazzled and anxious. **When your mind is constantly filled with noise, thoughts and ideas will escape like little birds flying away the moment you get too close.**

Creating quiet spaces to let our minds wander is important. What we're thinking about and how we mentally prepare before we enter that space is also important.

That's why you'll hear athletes, speakers, dancers, performers, and businesspeople of all kinds talking about visualization. They are entering a quiet space before they enter a very noisy and high-pressure space so that they may visualize what's about to take place and pay attention to what they know will be important. They're visualizing themselves being successful in the future as they sit and focus in the present.

Yet, if the athlete enters their game frantic, worried, and nervous, thinking they don't have what it takes, then the results are probably going to look very different. If they are telling themselves, "Look how big they are. Look how talented they are. Man, I have to guard number 3—he's so fast," then all they've focused on is all the ways they're going to fail. They're gonna play the game scared and number 3 is going to kick their butt because they already told themselves that.

I think the same applies to moms and dads trying to do a good job parenting their kids. It applies to students stepping into a classroom. It applies to real estate agents, financial advisors, tech engineers, salesmen, saleswomen, that if you've prepared yourself mentally, if you visualized what you want to do, if you don't come all frantic and all social-media saturated, reading headlines and bringing in all this junk, you are going to be able to step into your zone in your sphere much easier.

You can better operate on purpose toward your purpose if you're purposeful about preparing your mind beforehand.

When I'm going to speak at a large event, I'm usually pretty nervous. I'm anxious. I'm slightly afraid, no matter how many times I've done it before.

So before I go onstage, I'm usually walking around and praying, going over different lines in my head and what I'm going to say when I first walk out. I'm visualizing the audience laughing and being engaged. I've learned, in a sense, to be comfortable in the fear and in that nervousness. I've made peace with it, knowing that when I come up on the stage, my fear will turn into a certain kind of adrenaline that will almost help me think clearer when I'm speaking.

And yes, I'm still writing all this with some lavender bubbles around me, I'm not too proud to say. Honestly it's flowing so well that it almost feels like I'm not doing my due diligence as an author to sit there on a computer and beat myself up over every word, struggling to get the sentences to come out.

But when I'm in that quiet space, in the bath and in my mind, it feels like I'm having a conversation with you right now. And thankfully, for both our sakes, not while in the actual bathroom together! I'm just sharing my heart with you because I'm living it right now as I write, and I know the peace, energy, and excitement that it brings.

The Importance of Doing Physical Things in the Physical World

So much of our work and creativity is taking place on the computer, I think we need to make some intentional choices to do physical things in the physical world. To create and work in something that uses more of our senses.

For myself, I was spending so much time on the computer and writing as my main creative outlet that the computer was becoming this place of unrest and uncreativity for me.

Without making some big conscious long-term choice about what I should do it to fix this, I found myself being drawn to making things out of reclaimed wood. Never visualizing myself as a craftsman or "good with my hands" in that respect, I found such excitement and freedom in creating home goods with reclaimed wood. I started making coatracks, frames, and shelves out of old railroad spikes and big used bolts I'd find at Habit for Humanity's

Quiet spaces in our lives are sacred. We must treat them as such. It's like letting your mind enter a *wide-open meadow* to explore instead of keeping it wedged into the small confines of your phone.

—Paul Angone

Designed by Elizabeth Tenyer for *Listen to Your Day: The Life-Changing Practice of Paying Attention*

ReStore. Next thing you know, I'm seeing a sign for free fence wood and doing a U-turn so I could fill my Honda Civic Hatchback with as much old wood as I could.

I'm going to Goodwill and buying lamps for $1, then unwiring them and creating lamps out of copper pipe and reclaimed wood. I got so into this, I created another side business called "A King's Dream" where my wife and I would go to artisan fairs and set up an entire store in a parking lot. Selling my books, yes, but also selling all these things I had helped bring back to life with my hands. It was so incredibly rewarding and life-giving.

This creativity would then carry over into my writing and speaking. I remember one afternoon I was staining wood in my garage and started thinking about college graduation coming up. Next thing you know, I'm filming myself giving a whole graduation speech right off the top of my head. The creativity bubbled and flowed. My mind felt free to explore and try new things. I was giving myself permission to fail, experiment, and be creative in ways far beyond what I thought capable.

I think it is massively important for each one of us to find spaces of creativity and enjoyment in doing physical things in the physical world. Gardening has become another one of those things for me. Not only does your body need you to stop looking at a screen, get up, and get out of your chair, but your mind does too.

Quiet spaces in our lives are sacred. We need to treat them as such. It's like letting your mind enter a wide-open meadow to explore instead of keeping it wedged into the confines of your phone.

WHAT TO PAY ATTENTION TO TODAY:

I simply ask right now that you pay attention to what you're paying attention to in the margins of your day. I want you to notice all the times you grab your phone, turn on music, or flip on the

TV like a reflex to fill that awkward void. Always taking a break by jumping on your phone is not the most helpful or life-giving break you can take. Usually, it's quite the opposite. Try to catch yourself today, stop, and intentionally start thinking about positive activities you can do instead.

Write down ideas here of those positive activities you can do instead of escaping into your phone (e.g., exercising, crafting, gardening, praying, reading, cooking, etc.).

SIX

Paying Attention by Letting Your Mind Wander

Letting our minds wander seems like the exact opposite of paying attention, doesn't it?

Paying attention is about being present, right? So how can we be present if our minds are somewhere else? I'd argue that sometimes we need to be present in the moment we are in, paying attention to what is going on physically in front of us. Yet at other times we need to pay attention to what is going on internally. Our mind is wandering and we need to pay attention to where it is taking us.

As Joshua Shepherd noted in his article "Why Does the Mind Wander?" for the *Neuroscience of Consciousness*: "There is thus an apparent tension within mind wandering. When the mind wanders (at least unintentionally), agents are distracted from the current task, and performance suffers. But when the mind wanders, it tends to find non-occurrent goals the agent possesses, generating planning that could be beneficial."[1]

In other words, mind wandering can be beneficial or detrimental. Those times your mind wanders might be the pathway to answers, or it might be a distraction away from them. Sometimes it's more important for us to pay attention to the here and now, and other times it's more important to pay attention to the wandering path your mind has taken you down.

I'd argue that the two key variables that distinguish between the mind wandering being positive or negative are the level of importance of the task at hand and the thought the mind is wandering to.

Let me explain.

We've all experienced moments when mind wandering got us into trouble. Let's say you're listening to a professor, boss, or parent explain step-by-step instructions on how you are supposed to complete a big assignment or important task. Then all of a sudden you snap back into an instant "oh no" awareness when you realize your professor is standing right in front of you or your boss has stopped the meeting and is asking, "Are you paying attention?"

You gasp. Frantically look around. Your mind races. *How long was I zoned out? What words did I catch? Churchill. Bond allocation. ROI.* You were just listening, and in what felt like two seconds, you've somehow missed two minutes of important instruction. What happened? And what was so important that it literally took over your thoughts?

Your mind was engrossed with the last episode of *The Bachelor* that you just watched. You were sitting there wrestling with the unsettling observation of how William could've been so dumb to send Catalina home and keep Patricia!

Or you were thinking of your favorite football team and whether or not they should trade for that quarterback.

Or you were thinking about that broken relationship and the last conversation you had, dissecting it now for what was being said behind what was spoken.

Or that invention you've been working on, and you think you've just solved the problem that's been perplexing you for months.

You see, your mind is actively trying to solve a problem you had been paying attention to previously. Your mind is going back to your places of importance based on the thoughts you've been dwelling on in the past. It's like you've laid out bread crumbs, and when you get stuck, your mind will follow them back home.

For example, doing the dishes, taking a shower, walking in the park, lying down to sleep—these tasks have pretty low barriers of mental energy required to perform them. Thus, we are relaxed, yet focused. We are actively performing a task, yet our mind has the freedom to wander in ways that might have a beneficial result. Like a squirrel sitting on a fence before exploring the backyard, our mind is bored where it currently sits and is curious to explore what's "out there." And like that squirrel who has a desire to find a hidden nut or piece of fruit growing on a plant, our mind searches for answers pertaining to the questions that have been previously occupying our thoughts.

Mind wandering will happen. We can't necessarily stop it at all times, nor should we. Whether or not it's beneficial depends on the importance of the task that is in front of us and the thoughts that were occupying our mind beforehand. Basically, our mind will search for answers to what we have been paying attention to.

So two conclusions here when it comes to listening to our day. Sometimes we need to be paying attention to the present. Other times we need to pay attention to the past and future that our thoughts are revealing to us.

Mind Wandering and Microbreaks

Many psychologists recommend the idea of taking microbreaks at work to be more productive. In the report on the "Qualitative Study of Daydreaming Episodes at Work," a group of researchers concluded that "mind-wandering may be able to be used strategically to enhance work experience." The microbreak that the daydream provides can help to combat fatigue and strain during the day, because "it allows individuals to cognitively and affectively disengage from their work demands."[2]

As Boston College research professor Peter Gray wrote in *Psychology Today*,

> Dozens of experiments have shown that people who are stumped in solving certain kinds of problem are subsequently much more likely to solve the problem if they take a break. This is called the "incubation effect." . . . When we stop thinking consciously about the problem that we have been unable to solve, the unconscious mind takes the problem on and continues to work on it in some way. Suddenly, the mind hits a link that works, that solves the problem, and this awakens the conscious mind—"Aha, I see it now!"[3]

It's like you've given your mind a map to follow, and when you least expect it, your mind is going to explore the path to try and find the treasure (idea, conclusion, revelation, answer) at the end. So what kind of map are you giving your mind? What problems have you been paying attention to that your mind is now trying to solve?

The issue for many of us is that far too often our mental breaks are not productive—even counterproductive—because we use them to escape into other distractions. Your phone is probably not the mental break you need. In fact, your phone is breaking your mental focus.

You need those gaps in your day to take a break and do something, anything else you enjoy. Walking, gardening, cleaning, hiking, meditating, praying, exercising, crafting, or creating something with your hands—healthy activities that will allow your mind the space and time to wander, reflect, and think.

When you give your mind this space to breathe, it has a chance to reset. It allows your mind freedom to keep working the problem and finding the solution, even when you stopped actively processing the problem.

We need to create and protect intentional spaces in our day where our minds can rest and take a breath. Most days our minds are overly saturated. Like a sponge that is sitting in stagnant water, never allowed to dry and then be filled with something fresh.

> Most days our minds are overly saturated. Like a sponge that is sitting in stagnant water, never allowed to dry and then be filled with something fresh.

We are cognitively saturated, always filling our minds with new information when we have not yet understood, grasped, or grappled with the information we received the previous hour, day, week, or month.

What we focus our thoughts on throughout the day is what our mind will keep focusing on even when we're not actively paying attention to it. It's like there's a paying-attention ripple effect that takes place. We think we pay attention to something, and then once we shift our focus, it just goes away. But studies show that's not the case. Your mind does not simply let things go. So if you keep focusing your attention on the wrong things, then your mind is going to solve the wrong things.

Drama Llama

There's also a certain temptation toward drama, isn't there? Watching drama on TV through the latest reality TV show. Talking about the latest political drama with anyone who will listen. Embedding yourself in drama—some of your own doing and some that's not, yet you still join in for some reason.

I personally think we like focusing on other people's drama because we don't want to think about or solve our own. It's high avoidance.

We distract ourselves with drama. By attempting to solve other people's problems that we can't actually solve, nor have been asked to solve, nor can we do anything about, we are deceiving ourselves into thinking that we might find the solution to an issue that's not ours to solve.

Dissecting other people's problems is much sexier than doing something about our own.

The Jester

Let's talk about jesters. You know, like a Shakespearean jester who's doing his daily schtick in the castle. He's juggling balls. He's doing cartwheels down the hall. He's starting small fires that everyone can laugh at. The jester is this strange source of entertainment in this very serious place.

But what is the jester's goal? To make you laugh? Not really. That's the tool he uses, but that's not his real goal. His goal is to entertain and distract the king. But also to entertain and distract you from seeing the king.

His goal is to detain and divert you with entertainment so that you forget why you came to the castle with your pitchfork ready to tear some stuff up.

But let's say you're being taxed at 95 percent and you have one tin cup, half full, left of grain to feed your family of eleven. The jester could be pulling off tricks that would win him the golden buzzer on *Shakespeare's Got Talent*, but you'd still be charging through because you're not going to be deterred. Your goal is bigger than the jester's distractions, and you won't be detained by them.

Ask Yourself This One Question

Back to our non-Shakespearean day and age, I don't think we can simply tell ourselves, "Now, don't be distracted today and don't escape into your phone."

Sure, I think intentionally thinking about this and at least making the *conscious choice* to go on your phones instead of jumping on by reflex is step one.

When your mind is CONSTANTLY FILLED WITH NOISE, thoughts and ideas will escape like little birds flying away the moment you get too close

-PAUL ANGONE

But I think the second part is working on asking about and answering your "why" to start the day. Your goal has got to be bigger than the phone's siren call. Just like Odysseus. He was willing to let his men tie him to his boat so he wouldn't be lured off course. Because his goal was to make it home. His goal was bigger than any distraction, no matter how persuasive it may be.

You've got to have reasons why your time is more important than the time wasted elsewhere.

So what if we got into the daily habit of waking up and asking ourselves this one question: *What is the goal of my day?*

If you start by giving your mind a goal, then your mind will work on that goal throughout the day. You've given your mind a **path** and a **purpose** to the day. You've given yourself an intentional focus. If clarity feels fleeting in your life, start with this simple question to make your day, each day, more clear.

Goals and a vision for the future allow our mind and soul to see beyond the immediate reality into what's possible.

Maybe the goal is super specific and tied to a project like, you know, writing a book. Let's say I have a goal: "I want to write 2,000 words today." So throughout the day with that goal *in mind*, I will work toward accomplishing it. Now, if it's 10:30 a.m. and I find myself doing the infinite scroll on social media, my goal will give me more meaning to *why* I should stop. It feels more like a waste of time because I want to complete something specific with the time I have.

Or maybe your goal is big picture some days. Like . . .

I want to work toward physical and mental health today.

I want to love myself and love others well today.

I want to be open to hear what God is trying to tell me today.

Figure out your goal to start your day and then follow up that decision with an action that directly relates to the goal first thing in the morning.

For me, most mornings that means my action is trying to read the Bible and pray for ten minutes to start my day. I don't get on the phone first thing. I try to get up before the kids are full throttle. It doesn't always happen, so even if they are running around me fully throttled, I still do my best to start with this action to work toward my goal.

Worries and distractions don't have the same hold over me if I start my day by taking the time to focus on the eternal things of life that are important instead of constantly being overwhelmed by the blunt force of the present. "Set your mind and keep focused habitually on the things above [the heavenly things], not on things that are on the earth [which have only temporal value]" (Colossians 3:2 AMP).

Keep Your Why at the Center

If you keep your mind focused on your "why," when you experience those gaps throughout the day, you'll want to fill it with thoughts and actions that will meet that goal.

If you're at lunch and you're contemplating ordering that big burrito smothered with extra sour cream and a block of cheese shredded on top, you can think about your goal of physical and mental health. You can reflect from past experience how you're going to feel in an hour when you want to glue your head to the desk and never leave.

That's not going to help me toward my goal of physical and mental health. I should order that super salad instead.

Give your day a goal, give your mind a focus. This simple question makes paying attention purposeful. You're not just paying attention because some author is telling you that you should. You're paying attention for a purpose.

This is where the goals and your "why" need to be understood and at the center of building these small habits. Is your goal for today to be a better parent? Is it to be more productive at work? Is it to be more creative? Finish a project you've been hammering away at? Is it to have more energy and feel better about yourself?

If you keep your why at the center, it will make you pay attention to these small choices, because you will be actively weighing the consequences.

Do I stream another episode and wake up tired? Or do I choose to be a better parent for my kids? Do I choose that extra glass of wine? Or do I choose to speak coherently and creatively for my meeting tomorrow? Do I choose to make my phone the most important thing in my life? Or do I choose to make my faith, my spouse, and my kids more important?

You start weighing these choices and it feels like you've got a Twinkie on one side of the scale and ten gold bars on the other. The choice becomes much easier to make.

PRACTICE STARTING YOUR DAY
DEFINING YOUR WHY

When you wake up, don't jump on your phone. Instead, ask yourself what your goal is for the day. Write it down. Do this for the entire week.

Monday:

Tuesday:

Wednesday:

Thursday:

Friday:

Saturday:

Sunday:

DRAMA OBSERVATION

Are you being a Drama Llama? (This section is brought to you from my wife, Naomi.)

What drama in other people's lives do you keep gravitating toward? Write it down. Now draw a BIG FAT RED X over it and tell yourself you will no longer participate in that drama any longer. You will no longer "gather more information" about that drama, so that your mind will stop continuing to "solve" that drama, subconsciously distracting you from your own life and goals.

You will no longer be a "messenger" between parties within that drama, delivering more "information" to the participants. You will no longer be a "player" in that endless game. DECIDE out loud to not be involved in other people's drama. And remind yourself that it is a useless, wasteful vortex of pseudo satisfaction and pseudo problem-solving that adds zero worth to your life. Decide to step out of the world of drama and begin to focus on your OWN life goals. Begin today.

SEVEN

The Importance of Seminal Memories

We are past, present, and future beings. Memories of the past and goals for the future are crucial constructs needed to guide us in our present.

Memories give our mind and soul context for what we've learned, who we are, and where we want to go. As author and activist Wendell Berry poetically described in his essay "The Objective" for the documentary film *Look and See*, "With their many eyes opened only towards the objective, which they did not yet perceive in the far distance. Having never known where they were going. Having never known where they came from."[1]

Sometimes we are so focused on all our future objectives and directives, we lose sight of our context. We need to understand the experiences and memories that are directing us within each day, some of which we might not even realize. Paying attention to your day also means being aware of what I define as *seminal memories* that keep popping up in unexpected places. Let me explain.

Memories Are an Important Part of Being Present

Throughout the present day, we are consciously and unconsciously relying on memory to guide us safely. When we are present in the now, we are still constantly accessing the past. Our now is being viewed through thousands of those past experiences. Without memories, we'd be completely unable to function.

> Sometimes we are so focused on all our future objectives and directives, we lose sight of our context.

Growing up is a constant lesson in how to act and not act, learning what gets us rewarded and what gets us in trouble. We then build upon those memories, in both good and bad ways, to form our habits, actions, thoughts, and desires.

For example, driving a car is an active exercise in memory. A lack of remembering how to change gears while driving a stick shift or the best practices for driving on black ice during a storm can be the difference between life and death.

I once was driving too quickly in the rain on the 110 Freeway in Los Angeles. In a terrifying instant, my Honda Civic Hatchback, which weighed as much as a slightly damp box of matches, was hydroplaning and spinning from the far-left lane all the way across the highway and into the wall on the other side. Thankfully, I was not hurt badly, and a tow truck driver would be picking me up in a matter of moments. The drainage on the 110 Freeway was so bad that, as he explained to me like a guardian angel dressed in a tow driver's uniform, "I come to this corner during rainstorms and just wait for cars to spin out and crash."

Memories of spinning across the highway in the rain have forever shaped the way I drive. At first, I had to overcome a sense of PTSD. Whenever I slightly turned during the rain, my muscles would stiffen, my heart would race, and anxiety would overwhelm me. I had to work to overcome the feeling that "I'm going to crash" every time I drove in the rain.

But now, that memory is constantly directing my driving habits as I navigate in bad weather. Spinning across the highway once was and is one time too many for me.

Crashing in Relationships

Relationships and marriage provide great lessons in memories directing our present actions. Dating is a crash course in teaching us what to do, and not to do, in the context of a relationship.

We learn from foolish things we said in the past or ways we unknowingly hurt our spouse that we now are aware of in the present. It's the memory of the past that better helps us pay attention in the present. Relationships are constructed and contained in shared memories. Good and bad. It's hard to remove either.

So while we are living in the now, we are consciously and subconsciously pulling from memories to guide us in the best course of action. The now is not separate from the past; it's able to function because of the past.

The Terrible Loss of Memory

If you don't think that memories play this role, then merely spend an hour with someone who is stricken with the terrible disease of Alzheimer's. They lose their equilibrium. They lose all ability to operate in the now. For a period of time, Naomi and I lived with her grandmother who was losing her battle with the disease, and it was terrible to experience. Even going to the bathroom was a memory she could no longer access.

As famed author and professor of neurology Oliver Sacks said, "With Alzheimer's, it's common to lose one's memory for events and, in essence, to lose one's biography."[2]

To lose one's biography. That's powerful and scary. Without those memories, you don't know what page you're on. You can't function. Memories play a crucial, constant role in living in the now.

Seminal Memories

Yet, I don't want to just focus on the memories that guide our daily actions. I want to focus here on what I call *seminal memories*.

Seminal memories are what I define as core experiences unique to each one of our stories that have formed a deep part of our identity. They are the recurring memories that we keep being drawn to. The ones we keep noticing in unexpected places. Why do they keep showing up?

Seminal memories are our meaning makers. These core experiences formed a deep impression, like the way a tree adds rings each year.

What we need to pay attention to here is what our seminal memories are and how they are informing our present and future goals.

Seminal memories find a way to continually pop up in front of us—in "random" times throughout our day, in our daydreams, or as we drift to sleep. As we sip our coffee or go on a walk. As we see certain sights, smell the orange blossom from a tree, hear a certain song, we are transported to a place and time. The amazing discovery in Alzheimer's patients who have lost their memory is how songs from the past can help them recover their sense of self. As Sacks says, "Personal memories are embedded to some extent in things like music . . . the past which is not accessed in any other way is embedded in the music."[3]

Maybe this seminal memory is a good one, maybe a bad one, but in some way it keeps coming back to our current view for a reason. These memories have deeply informed our identity, in positive and negative ways. Yet, most times we don't see this and we don't understand it.

Sometimes we might need to elicit the help of the people closest to us to better understand the seminal memories that clearly played a huge role in forming who we are.

When Memories Give Context to the Present

My wife and I had been together for fifteen years before I noticed she had recently been bringing up two seminal memories from a similar timeframe in her life. One good and one bad. And yet, it wasn't until we paid attention to them and stopped to discuss them that we realized what both of these seminal memories were telling her about the way she was experiencing her day.

The first memory Naomi keeps being drawn back to is her middle school days and really discovering her love for the Lord. Faith plays an important role in our family, and especially for my wife in her identity and core beliefs. She kept going back to that place of her first love where she remembers coming home from school, going to her room, and just worshiping the Lord for hours and hours. Not your typical afternoon for an emerging middle school teen!

The next year she and her sisters would be uprooted from their school, community, and church on the East Coast to be moved by her parents to San Diego across the country. But first, by means of living in Tijuana, as her parents worked on making the full transition.

She recalled pleading and crying, along with her three sisters, to her dad not to move them. She remembered the sense of being uprooted from that safe, quiet space to a place of fear, unknowns, and chaos as she began a new life in Tijuana and then San Diego. It was in this season that she lost the ability to escape to that room to sing her heart out to the Lord, and instead learned a survival mechanism of escaping into her own thoughts and striving to figure out life on her own. She learned to escape into a place that she could control as her life felt out of control.

Both of these memories kept coming to the surface twenty-seven years after she experienced them, as we went through some turbulent weeks of travel, a sense of being uprooted, possible COVID infections, looking for a new home, and basically every chaotic life thing that could be thrown at us in a short period of time.

Memories are our meaning makers

- Paul Angone

Fear and anxiety were gripping her tight and not letting go. We talked about those two memories and the feeling that she was experiencing of God inviting her back into that room of peace and comfort. As we talked, and as she prayed, she could begin to see and feel how this current situation was not the same. She could heal from that seminal, scarring memory of being uprooted and moved across the nation into a prolonged, difficult season for her family, where she subconsciously walked away from her trust in God. She could go back to that room, back to a loving embrace and peace in her soul. Anxiety and fear did not need to have the death grip that they were having. And those seminal memories were a way her mind and soul were still searching to find a place to finally conquer her mountain.

After wrestling with this for days, I could see her start breathing again. Seeing and understanding these seminal memories helped her heal and operate from a different, deeper, more peaceful place in the present. Within her current circumstances, God opened a door for her to walk back through to that place of peace, joy, and trust, with a different response than she had in the past. One of faith instead of fear. One that said, "I can see now that no matter the circumstance, I know that all things will work together for the good for those who trust in him."

PRACTICE DEFINING
YOUR SEMINAL MEMORIES

You see, no self-help book can give you the exact formula for leading a successful, fruitful, meaningful life. A book can, and should, help you lay the groundwork. But how you build the walls and construct the house needs to be based on the framework you have been building your life upon.

If we pay attention to what we deem our greatest successes and also the most difficult things we've gone through, we can better understand all kinds of crucial components of ourselves. Our strengths, the skills we enjoy operating in, our values, and often-times what we would call our passion and our purpose. All of these are deeply embedded in our greatest triumphs and tragedies, and they are informing our current day and who we are *being* in the present.

What are your Top 3 to 5 Greatest Triumphs? (Successes that were extremely meaningful and impactful to you.)

What are your Top 3 to 5 Great Tragedies? (Don't have to be of Shakespearean nature, but just hard things you've gone through and still think about in your memories throughout your day and had to work on overcoming.)

Now let's pay attention to the patterns here. Do you see any connection points in your triumphs and tragedies? Do you see the same skills and strengths popping up in your greatest successes? Do you see certain what you consider to be core principles at play?

I ask about tragedies as well, because these have deeply formed our identity just as much, if not more, than our triumphs. Either this seminal memory of a tragedy is something you're still healing from, need to heal from, or have healed from as you recover from the lies this hard event infused into your present identity. Oftentimes this is what a therapist is helping you uncover—those hard events of the past that you need to see and possibly define differently so that you can better function now.

These tragedies from the past will not become helpful in our present and future if the thought of them still fills us with overwhelming amounts of guilt, shame, or regret. We will continually feel sick if we are constantly consuming these emotions. It will be difficult to see the blessings of today if we are constantly brought down by the burdens of the past.

But these tragedies can become your superpower. Your greatest pain can become your greatest passion. You know in a deeply personal way what it's like to go through something hard and now you have a passion to help others going through a similar thing. You have a resolve, understanding, and an empathy in a specific area that is unique to you because of the role that seminal memory has played in your life.

Now, as you listen to and see your day, can you see how these seminal memories are playing out in your day-to-day actions and beliefs? Today, whenever you're reading this, I want you to look at your day through the lens of your seminal memories. Are you currently incorporating the skills and strengths that you saw pop up in these memories? Are you living by the values that you have identified as important to you?

Now I want to take this exercise one step further. I want you to try to identify seminal memories that you have not already written down. I want you to spend the next day paying attention to the memories that pop into your consciousness throughout the day.

Over the next few days, pay attention to the memories that come to your mind. Good or bad. Seemingly insignificant or immediately profound. Write them all down here. Fill up these pages. Ask a few people who are close to you where they have seen you most alive. Ask them what memories they hear you talk about the most.

You can be present in your day only if you understand your past. Your past, your memories, are directly contributing to your being present in the now. Pay attention to them. See them. Hear what they're saying. Write them down.

Thoughts from the Bathtub on "Life Happening to Us"

Life just happens to you, so you might as well just let it take its course.

That's a lie.

Sure, unexpected things happen all the time to all of us. But life is how you respond to them.

Of the best things that happen in your life, 99.99 percent of them won't happen at the time or place or in the way that you expected. So the next time things don't go as planned, maybe that was the exact plan after all.

Your success and fulfillment in life then comes down to a combination of thousands of choices, thoughts, and decisions you make when things aren't going as planned.

If we continue to believe the lie that life just happens to us and we are powerless to make wise, smart decisions, what's the point of paying attention and choosing the right path out of wisdom?

If none of it matters, then something is really the matter. Your thoughts matter. What you pay attention to matters. The thoughts you choose to dwell on matter.

If you keep believing that life just happens to you, then you are removing all responsibility and accountability for your actions.

Sure, we can't control every detail. We can't control every factor. Life doesn't always work out like a mathematical formula or a science experiment, where if you put in these elements, at these exact amounts,

> **Of the best things that happen in your life, 99.99 percent of them won't happen at the time or place or in the way that you expected. So the next time things don't go as planned, maybe that was the exact plan after all.**

then you will get the same result every time. But you can study the amounts, you can learn from past experiments, so that you can do it better the next time.

So yes, life may feel like it happens to us, but the real question becomes, What will happen to the life that you have yet to live?

Will you intentionally choose to choose? Will you ask for guidance, wisdom, and truth when you don't know the answers? Will you surrender the need to control every detail and trust that things will work out the way they are supposed to if you keep choosing the right path?

Will you pay attention to your gut? Choosing what your gut knows is right over what you know is wrong? Will you think about the choices you're making today, or will they all just be knee-jerk reactions? Will you choose the path of wisdom, or will you choose the path of foolishness?

I'm telling you from experience as one who has taken far too many steps on the path of foolishness, where it leads is much less enjoyable than you expect. You might think there's a party waiting for you at the end, when instead it's incredible lostness and darkness. You sprinted down the path of foolishness, thinking you had no time to waste. Then, you spend the next two, five, ten years trying to retrace your steps back to where you started.

Pursue wisdom now. Walk down that path. Pay attention to it. Lady Wisdom is calling out to anyone who chooses to listen. She will lead to a life lived well. There's ripe fruit galore lining that path—the fruit of knowing who you are and being at peace on the path, even when you're not exactly sure where that path is taking you.

For me, I know I can't fully stay on this path alone. There's surrender on the path of wisdom. I'm far too weak and foolish to think I can manage the journey by myself.

Personally, this means when things feel like they are spinning out of control, I can ask God for help holding me up. I can trust and thank the God who is in control. Even when I do make the wrong choices, there is grace and mercy to help get it right. This doesn't give me complete latitude to willingly make wrong choices, but it does give me a do-over, a hand up, a loving embrace from a Father who says, "Let me help you do this better the next time."

Sure, life happens. Every day it does. But it is our daily responses, choosing right over wrong, that make life what it is for us.

EIGHT

Physical Component to the Mind

Have you ever driven through a dense fog before? Where you can't see anything in front of you? So you drive at a snail's pace, because you don't want your day to end up at the bottom of a cliff you never saw coming.

Let me come clean to you, I stayed up too late last night streaming something. Now it's 11:13 a.m. the next day and it feels like I've been driving through that dense fog all morning, one hand on the wheel while the other is on my laptop, trying to type. Not exactly a conducive combination to writing poetic and profound prose. I'm just trying not to crash the proverbial car.

Let me go lie down and think more about this during a quick three-hour nap . . .

I messed up and now I'm paying for it.

I bring this up because obviously, there are some basic physical components to paying attention to our day. Levels of self-discipline and self-care go hand in hand to hearing the ideas, revelations, truths, and nuances each day is trying to tell us.

If you had a pet monkey and didn't let it sleep, fed it nothing but junk food, gave it an iPhone, and let it drink a few shots of Jack Daniels night after night, well, that little guy is not going to be ready to perform many circus tricks anytime soon. They'd be calling animal control on you.

Same with our minds. Should we really be surprised on too many of *those* days that we can't seem to think straight?

We can't keep thinking we can neglect our minds and bodies, and then keep expecting them to perform for us. There's a level of self-control and self-discipline that gives us the freedom and focus to pay attention. When we pretend that self-discipline and impulse control don't play a role in any of this, we're making each day much harder on ourselves than we have to.

We can be intentional about our choices or continue to be smacked in the head with the consequences.

The First Promise to You

What if, right now, I could offer you something that will radically change your life? It will help you think clearer. It will provoke strategies, ideas, and energy like you've never experienced before. It's nearly magical, yet it's scientifically proven to help you pay attention.

What is this magic brew, you ask?

Sleep. At night. When you should be sleeping.

It's radical. It's wild. It's the most regenerative and restorative potion we could give ourselves. And it's free. It involves lying down in the most comfortable spot in our entire house. But we keep avoiding it.

We need it. We know we need it. Yet we keep sacrificing it. For what?

To binge-watch another episode? To go down that rabbit hole of memes or an hour's worth of Reddit threads about something you didn't know you were interested in until seven minutes ago?

Sleep is so extremely important and valuable. But it's like we're bankrupting ourselves, standing outside our house, and giving away $20 bills to anyone who walks by. Then we look at our bank balance and wonder why it's drawing a negative.

We don't seem to have enough sleep, yet we keep freely giving it away.

Sure, sleep doesn't always come easy for some of us. There are mental and physical blocks that can keep us from this blessed event.

If young babies and toddlers get thrown in the mix of your day and night, now you've got monkeys coming into your bed at 3:00 a.m. Waking you up. Asking you to go get their water bottle that they just left back at their bed. Telling you they had a bad dream and their left leg hurts. Or was it their right arm? Oh, now it's their left foot . . . Then after this thirty-minute circus and the moment has finally come for that sanctity of sleep to reenter the room, out of nowhere your two-year-old whispers, "Daddy . . . *Daddy* . . . do you remember orca whales?"

Yes, all of this, exactly how I wrote it, happened to me last week. And every other night, with some slight variations, for the past ten years it feels!

Side note: If toddlers were more strategic, they could really rack up some decent middle-of-the-night bribes.

Do you want me to get you a pony tomorrow? I will buy you that cotton candy machine. Yes, you can get that tattoo when you're sixteen and have my car. Whatever you want. Just, please, please, sleep.

Your Brain Cells Act Drunk

Dr. Itzhak Fried, professor of neurosurgery at David Geffen School of Medicine at UCLA and Tel Aviv University, did a study on sleep deprivation with twelve epilepsy patients who had electrodes planted in their brains. "We discovered that starving the body of sleep also robs neurons of the ability to function properly. This leads to cognitive lapses in how we perceive and react to the world around us."[1]

WE MUST *fight* TO PAY ATTENTION. TO THE _right_ THINGS. TO THINGS OF *worth* AND *meaning*. TO CHANGING THE WAY WE _see_ OUR DAY SO THAT WE CAN TRULY SEE IT FOR THE *gift* IT IS.

— Paul Angone

Designed by @jasminegreen
for *Listen to Your Day*

Basically, as patients got tired, they couldn't pay attention. Similar to drinking too much, patients experienced a lapse in time from visually seeing something to their brain cells then becoming aware of what they were seeing.

Another study on the lack of sleep and corresponding anxiety levels found that "78 percent of all participants in the sleep-deprived condition reported an increase in anxiety, confirming a robust impact of sleep loss on the escalation of anxiety in healthy individuals."[2]

Sleep is so necessary to enable us to pay attention and focus on what's important. Not to mention some other factors like to reduce chances for obesity, speed up metabolism, help fight depression, reduce risk of some cancers, fight against Alzheimer's, *yada yada yada*. You know, sleep helps with a few things.

So if you're having trouble sleeping, or you're consistently making choices keeping you from a good night's sleep, you need to fight for it. Ask for medical or mental help if you feel like this is an impossible task. Don't take your phone to bed with you. Find a routine that helps relax you and gets you ready to sleep well.

A consistent lack of sleep is like drugging your brain cells and then asking them to recite the Gettysburg Address at 8:00 a.m. It's not an optimal combo. Our attention will continually be shattered like a piggy bank with our cents and sense spilling all over the floor until we welcome some sweet sleep into our beds.

Water, Real Food, Exercise

Things like water, good food, and exercise are really helpful as well to give your mind a fresh crispness like a cucumber just picked from the vine. All the sugar and refined foods that fill up too many of our diets are like marinating our minds in black tar, then asking them to run a race.

Believe you me, I'm not some highly disciplined person who's cranking out marathons while talking to a group of venture capitalists to invest in my latest billion-dollar idea. I feel more struggle-fest than motivated most days. (Cue toddler coming into my bed again last night and crying hysterically because she wanted her shoes on at 3:00 a.m. And she would not take no for an answer! This really happened. Ask my wife. I'm too tired to make these things up.)

But again, making these small, consistent choices toward health is not only helping our physical health. It's helping our mental and emotional health as well. It will bring a heightened awareness, an ability to see and comprehend things you have not noticed in the past. Just break it down into small, daily, consistent choices.

It's like Farming 101. If your soil is dry and stripped of nutrients, you'll be growing nothing but weeds. Every garden of Eden starts with a healthy, vibrant soil. How are you replenishing your soil?

Let's focus on making your soil vibrant with life so that you can focus. Sleep, exercise, water, and good whole foods are like injecting your mind with superpowers.

I'm not trying to oversimplify this. I'm just trying to make it a lot less complicated than we act like it is.

Do it for your body. Your heart. Your mind. A mantra of today's culture is do what makes you happy. Well, I'm telling you sleep, drinking water, exercise, and eating real food are going to make you happier in the long run than any other mood-altering drug, alcohol, road trip, party, or movie will ever be able to produce.

> It is a wild contradiction in our culture that so much of what we prop up as making us happy is so bad for our long-term health.

Give your mind a truckload of nutrients and watch the amazing things that grow. It is a wild contradiction in our culture that so much of what we prop up as making us happy is so bad for our long-term health.

Lasting happiness comes from consistently making smart choices toward health, not away from it.

NINE

What Paying Attention to Your Excitement and Anxiety Can Tell You

Wow, there is a lot to be anxious about these days, isn't there?

One little bite of a social media feed can be a fire hose of fear, worry, and anxiety that will spray you in the face before you even have a chance to look away. All of a sudden you feel drenched in anxiety before you even roll out of bed.

We can't fully escape fear, worry, and anxiety. But we can work on seeing them for what they are and responding accordingly.

Over the years, I've learned the power and importance of paying attention to my anxiety. This statement already feels counterintuitive, because who wants to give their anxiety more time than it already takes from us? But it's in the understanding and defining of my anxiety that I'm able to give it less power over me than before. If I can stare my anxiety in the face and see it for what it is, I can better understand it. Then by understanding it, I can think about what that anxiety is trying to tell me.

Our anxiety is telling us a lot. But if we never understand what the source of the anxiety is, then it becomes this all-encompassing, looming, faceless force that has its way with us. Your anxiety might be revealing to you something incredibly important about your soul values that you didn't understand before.

I'm not trying to oversimplify the battle against anxiety and all the steps one might need to take to combat or limit it. All I want to address here is a tool for paying attention to anxiety in a different way. Instead of seeing anxiety as simply something to mitigate and escape from, what if we looked it in the face and see what it has to tell us. Maybe if we pay attention to our anxiety and define it, it then in turn can give us much needed clarity for our day.

Full of Anxiety

We're all probably anxious at some point throughout the day. We all have worries and fears. Sometimes they're at "hurtling down a steep sidewalk on a skateboard without any idea how to stop" kind of levels. Other days, they are a low beat, like background music you are feeling while not hearing a single word.

But what if you defined your anxiety? For me, this does two things: it reveals to me both what is important for me to pay attention to and what is not.

For example, I've had too many instances than I can count where I'm feeling anxious, yet I don't even know what I'm feeling anxious about. It's this looming anxiety that is affecting me, yet I can't see the source. So I stop, think, and start paying attention to the things that came directly in front of me that I did not recognize as possible causes. I start retracing my steps to find the source of anxiety.

Was it the conversation I just had with my wife? No, that was good.

Was it what I just ate? No, I feel good about the choice of a salad and hummus.

Was it being on my phone and seeing that post from my friend about the big deal he just closed? Hmm . . . no, I don't think that was it. I feel excited for him and I'm totally content not working in his field and putting in his hours to make that deal happen. *But I feel I'm close to finding it . . .*

Was it being on my phone, looking at my own post, and seeing how many likes I got? Or in my estimation, how few likes I got? Bingo! Rod, tell him what he's won . . .

Now, I've defined my anxiety. I know the source. I can see it for what it is and come to the conclusion, in this instance, that my anxiety is stemming from paying attention to the wrong thing. I can talk through it and tell myself all the things I *know*. I shouldn't be focusing on how many likes I got or didn't get. My value and worth shouldn't be coming from this perceived instant validation.

My anxiety is showing me that I've put too much importance on something that is not worth the weight of that kind of importance. Now that I've defined it, I can move back toward paying attention to what is important. I can choose to not focus on my follower counts and focus on what actually matters. I can put the proper weight in the proper places, instead of choosing to fill up my daily wheelbarrow with cement blocks that I have no purpose for and then wondering why everything feels so heavy!

Anxiety and Values

On the other hand, anxiety can reveal to me that I'm *not* paying attention to what is important.

Can understanding your anxiety be a way to helping you understand your values? I believe it can. Sometimes in understanding our anxiety, it becomes an important lens to understanding our soul values.

So what do I mean by soul values?

Soul values are the core principles that guide your actions and decision-making processes.

The issue for many of us is that we don't exactly know what our top soul values are. Like we do with anxiety, we have this looming notion of what our soul values might be, but we're not exactly sure. We know they're there. But we can't quite put a finger on them.

> Soul values are the core principles that guide your actions and decision-making processes.

We see the forest around us every day, but we haven't noticed the details on the trees in years.

So how can anxiety help point me toward my values? Once I define the anxiety, I might be able to better see that my anxiety is stemming from a contradicted soul value.

This realization can lead to conviction and then a conscious choice to change my actions and thoughts to better align. I'm not putting enough importance on that which I hold important. Sometimes what we might confuse for anxiety is actually conviction.

Is It Anxiety? Or Is It Conviction?

For example, let's say I find myself feeling consistently anxious in the morning. I just can't seem to start the day off right. I get up. Check my phone. Make coffee. Try and eat something before I'm flying out of the door to fight traffic and make it to work.

I show up to work already feeling stressed, anxious, and wishing I could just go back to bed.

All right, what's making me anxious in the mornings? Could it be something to do with a soul value that's not being met? Let's say I put my spiritual faith and having a right relationship with God as my number one value. Is anything about the way I'm starting my day confirming what I say is my number one value?

Or is it a direct contradiction? I used to get up, make some coffee, read my Bible, journal, and pray before I did anything else. It felt like such a right way to start my day. But gosh, with four kids, who has time for that? God surely understands that I just don't have the time.

Well, is it a problem that I don't have the time, or is it a problem that it's not important enough for me to make the time?

Ouch.

If it is important enough to me to make the time, then I need to start making some conscious choices to see it happen.

A healthy morning routine is so important. I lost the routine, and now I feel like I'm starting the day with my heart tied behind my back.

That might mean going to bed earlier, so that I'm not dragging myself out of bed and barely making it to work on time.

Is my phone one of my top soul values? No. So why would I start my day with something that is depleting me the moment I wake up? That feels contradicting and obviously draining. Why do I spend so much of my choice time throughout the day paying attention to something that I wouldn't rank in my top ten soul values?

Too many of us, myself included, contradict our soul values first thing in the morning and the last thing at night. Then we wonder why we feel fragmented.

Tracing my anxiety back, I gain a better understanding that it's a conviction tied to a soul value that's not being met, so now I can make wiser choices toward convergence of my soul. Instead of continually being fragmented and then wondering why I feel so busted up every morning.

I can ask myself, Is there life in this decision? Does this choice feel life-giving to me or life-taking?

Some might refer to this thought process as listening to your conscience or your gut. If your soul values are constructed from a faith perspective, you might see this process as listening to God's Spirit who is actively guiding you in the big and very small details of your day.

FAR TOO OFTEN
THE THINGS WE
PAY SO MUCH
ATTENTION TO
MEAN SO VERY
LITTLE IN THE
IMPORTANT, GRAND
SCHEME OF THINGS.
- PAUL ANGONE -

In understanding and defining your soul values, you have a better framework from which to make your daily decisions.

As you begin to understand your values and define them, you can pay attention to them throughout the day. You can begin to see them. In those moments you feel anxious or excited, you can begin connecting those emotions to your soul values.

You can make better decisions toward convergence instead of fragmentation.

> In understanding and defining your soul values, you have a better framework from which to make your daily decisions.

Paying Attention to Anxiety and Energy at Work

Sometimes we learn the most in the jobs we like the least. That's not the most engaging teacher, but it teaches us quite a bit about what we like and don't like.

I think many of our disconnects and angst at work don't come from a skill set issue, they come from a contradicted soul value. Something's missing. You don't even know what that something is, but it's making you feel anxious.

You might even be making good money. Have good relationships with coworkers. Yet you still find yourself feeling anxious at different points in the day. What's missing? Or maybe, what value is not being met? It's something to pay attention to.

You love so much of what you do, and yet there's something that's making you feel anxious. What is it?

You sit down to think about it, and you start recognizing when your anxiety begins spouting like a broken fire hydrant. It's because you're continually being asked to work later and later in the day.

As you think of your values and what is most important to you, spending quality time with your family is an apparent soul value in your life. It ranks at the top. So no matter how fulfilling your job feels, it doesn't override the feeling that success at your job is not a higher value for you than your family.

Now your anxiety has revealed to you the hierarchy of your soul value system, and you can begin to make intentional choices and decisions accordingly. You can talk to your boss and ask for their input on how you can still do an incredible job for the team but have that quality time to spend with your family.

As you trace back the source of your anxiety, it can reveal to you a deep well that you never really noticed before.

Then on the other hand, your energy and excitement level can also pull the curtain up and reveal to you what you value most. When you feel like you're in your "sweet spot" at work, you're probably utilizing strengths that align with your skill set. Also the "why" behind what you're doing probably also aligns with your top soul values. You feel at peace and ready to fully lean in because you're complementing your top values instead of contradicting them. You don't feel like you're working against yourself but that all parts are working toward the whole.

> The success sweet spot is simply a place where your skill set is working in unison with your soul values. They are dancing together in the same direction.

The success sweet spot is simply a place where your skill set is working in unison with your soul values. They are dancing together in the same direction.

Values are a crucial piece that bring peace but also productivity. It's hard to do something with skill and proficiency that you know is secretly contradicting the values you hold most important. Like filling a helium balloon up but having nothing to tie it down to Sure, it might fly high and far, but in the end, for what or for how long? Soon it will all explode in shriveled pieces because there was nothing anchoring it down.

As you go about your day at work, school, or home, I want you to pay attention to your anxiety and your excitement. Define your anxiety and your excitement. Both the negative emotion of anxiety and the positive emotion of energy and excitement can reveal to us our soul values—either by understanding how our values are being contradicted by our actions or how they are complementing them.

What are each telling you about the level of importance you are, or should not be, placing on certain parts of your day? What are your anxiety and excitement telling you about your top soul values and the principles you hold highest when living your life?

You see, we all have a value system. No matter what. But most of us have never defined what that system looks like. So when things are running smoothly or when everything is broken down on the side of the road, we don't know what went right, or wrong, because we never took time to pay attention to either.

Look at the questions in the chart below and see what clarity and definition you discover through what your anxiety and excitement are telling you.

Anxiety—Contradicting your soul values
Energy and Excitement—Complementing your soul values

ANXIETY	ENERGY & EXCITEMENT
What exactly are you feeling (emotions, thoughts, physically)?	What exactly are you feeling (emotions, thoughts, physically)?

ANXIETY	ENERGY & EXCITEMENT
What were you doing that led to this feeling?	What were you doing that led to this feeling?
Is this showing you something important that you should be focusing on?	Is this showing you something important that you should be focusing more on?
Or is this showing you something that's unimportant in your life that you shouldn't be focusing on?	Is there a skill set or soul value that you are complementing that led to this excited feeling?
Is there a soul value that you could be contradicting that led to this anxious feeling?	

TEN

Paying Attention to People

Each day contains ideas, revelations, and clarity just waiting to be uncovered. Each day is rich with meaning, even in the mundane. **Each day is an invitation to pay attention, to be alive in it instead of waiting for "some day" in the future when we will start really living our lives to the fullest.**

As we continue forward on this quest to be active participants in listening to and hearing what your day is telling you, it would be a big miss to not discuss one of the most constant and consistent components that each day will possess. The people in each day with us.

One specific place that we've lost the ability to pay attention— possibly more than anywhere else—is paying attention to each other.

Many of us would say the most important things in our lives are our friends and family. But do our day-to-day actions back this sentiment up? How does the way we pay attention to each other, or fail to do so, tell the most important people in our lives what we truly think and feel about them?

We might even say we love someone. But do we pay attention to them? In actions and reality? On a given day with this person in the room, have we paid more attention to this person or our phone? Throughout our day, every day, we'll be around people. If we're going to properly listen to our day, sometimes we will need to do a better job listening to the people involved in it.

We need to stop networking like machines and start *relationshipping* like human beings. But I think as a cultural whole, there's definitely a trend toward becoming lazy, uninterested, or completely unaware conversationalists.

"Give me your undivided attention." We know the phrase. We've heard the phrase. Yet, in reality our attention is fragmented.

During a conversation, far too often we want to speak, but we don't want to listen. We want to take so much out of a conversation, but we want to give so little.

We laud ourselves as amazing multitaskers, yet sometimes this simply means we're very effective at being effectively distracted.

You can't focus on a person but busy yourself with something else while the one speaking to you wonders if you're listening at all.

Every day is filled with relationships and interactions with people where we can learn so much about each other, ourselves, and living life well through our daily interactions. But we seem to be losing our sense of personal connection to each other. Why is that and what can we do about it?

The Importance of Being Seen and Heard

In today's world, where so many of us are craving to be seen and heard, nothing can have such a profound effect on someone's life as feeling like they are known. Even if by just one person. How can someone feel known by you if they feel you're rarely paying attention to them?

Nothing, absolutely nothing, can create more meaningful relationships for you right now than your ability to pay attention to others. Your kids. Your spouse. Dating partner. Your parents. Colleagues. Your boss. Your client or the person you're trying to make a client. Your teacher or your students. Your friends. If people in your life don't feel you're paying attention to them most of the time, then they're probably also not going to feel like you really care. No doubt that statement seems pretty basic, but we need to address it nonetheless, because I have a sneaking suspicion that many of us feel we could be loving others better than we are.

The Washoe County School District on the outskirts of Reno realized they needed to make a change as their graduation rates were hovering around 55 percent in the 2010s. What could they do to improve their graduation numbers, produce less behavioral problems, and even curb the rising epidemic of suicide amongst young people?

In 2012, the school district initiated their "Every Child, by Name and Face, to Graduation" social and emotional focused-learning program. The core of the program is challenging teachers to not only know the name and the face of their students but to know something personal about them, to ask students questions about their interests, hobbies, and even the challenges they are experiencing so that each student feels like they had at least one meaningful connection with a teacher every day.[1]

In 2010 the county graduation rate was 55 percent. In 2019, they hit a record number 86 percent and could have reached their goal of 90 percent graduation rate by 2020 if an epidemic hadn't stepped in and stolen their momentum.

Seventh-grade science teacher Chris Ewald put it best: "It's harder for students to feel valued in a learning environment without that connection to the teacher. . . . We are developing trust and loyalty, and then students are no longer a piece of data, but a real human being."[2]

Does this idea translate to a work environment? I think it does.

Part of my career is speaking to leaders and CEOs from all different kinds of industries on how to do a better job retaining, engaging, communicating with, and connecting to younger professionals. I'm working on a separate book that goes into much further detail on this subject, tentatively titled *The Adult Table: How to Lead, Engage, and Build Trust Equity with the Next Generation*. One of the things I stress is how important it is that leaders create personal connection with their people. Leaders paying attention to their staff pays huge dividends.

Wharton School of Business conducted a study around mentorship and found that those in mentoring relationships had a 20 percent higher retention rate than those who had none. But this wasn't just for the younger people being mentored. The higher retention rates also rang true for the older professionals as well. Both young and old were finding more value through paying attention to and having a personal connection with just one other person.

If employees feel seen, heard, and known, they are more likely to stay. Basically, pay attention to your people. They are the most valuable resource you have. Not only are the costs of hiring and training new talent astronomical, but the amount of organizational knowledge that will be lost when employees don't feel seen or heard is something an organization cannot afford.

Employees don't want to be treated like a cog. Nothing will make an employee feel more insignificant than if they sense that leadership doesn't care about them as people, that they care only about their production.

Employees think it should matter that they want their work and their lives to matter. I instruct leaders to stop treating younger employees like they should be sitting at the kids table, where they aren't trusted with knives so they're using plastic sporks and Styrofoam cups. I encourage leaders to invite their staff to sit at the adult table, where they can feel seen and a part of the bigger conversation. Even if leaders preface the invitation to a big meeting by instructing the younger staff member that they don't need to say anything at the meeting—you just want them to be your eyes and ears. You just want them to be there. Right then, that staff member will feel seen and important.

Pretty simple—if people feel like you pay attention to them and treat them like a person, they are more likely to trust you, feel connected, and stay.

Paying Attention to Your Spouse or Partner

For too many of us, our spouse can feel like the well-loved couch in the living room. It's always there, so you don't think much of it. You don't pay much attention to it. Then all of a sudden, one day you look at it and really see it: *Wow, it's got a lot of stains, wear, and tear on it. I should have been taking better care of this!*

We stop seeing the couch because it's just always there. Hence the phrase "absence makes the heart grow fonder." Once the person finally leaves for a bit, you start realizing all the things they are and do that you've taken for granted. But isn't it a bit messed up that we can appreciate the person we're with only once they're finally gone?!

Do you think many spouses would want to be described like the old couch in the living room that everyone sits on? Probably not. Yet, that's how many of our relationships start to feel. We stop noticing each other, and I believe that leads to serious problems.

So how do we start changing some patterns in the ways we pay attention to our spouse and loved ones? How do we start focusing on the good in them rather than on all the things that annoy, bug, or straight-up drive us crazy about them?

The Love Languages

Take *The Five Love Languages* by Gary Chapman. This book sells more copies every year than the previous one, with sales now over 17 million copies with the various spinoff books. You have probably heard about the concepts of the book if you have not already read it, but basically Dr. Chapman's core tenet is that not all people receive love the same way. We have different "love languages," like quality time, acts of service, physical touch, words of affirmation, and receiving gifts.

But really, these five love languages and your ability to effectively express love to those around you boils down to your level of awareness and your ability to pay proper attention to the person you're with. You're paying attention to their needs and how they receive love, and then you're acting according to that awareness every day. If you're not paying attention to your spouse at this base level, how will you be able to see or understand what they are feeling, thinking, or wrestling with?

> Your ability to love your spouse or dating partner well is directly hinging on your ability or inability to pay attention to them.

Your ability to love your spouse or dating partner well is directly hinging on your ability—or inability—to pay attention to them. If your spouse feels like you are paying more attention to everything else in life but them, then the relationship will start to feel bankrupt.

You can't pay attention to your spouse for five minutes a day and then expect the relationship to feel rich.

Highest Reasons for Divorce

Obviously marriage issues are complex, but if you look at various research, it's probably not too big of a surprise that some consistent issues for divorce emerge, such as problems with "communication, incompatibility, and commitment."[3]

While I'm not saying that marriage complexities and issues can be fixed with a Magical Marriage Wand, I am wondering how much less of an issue our "communication, incompatibility, and commitment" problems would be if each person made the simple choice and "commitment" to work on paying attention to their spouse. Not blaming them. Or ignoring them. But sitting down and paying attention to them.

Each Day is an invitation to pay attention, to be ALIVE in it instead of WAITING for "Some Day"

—PAUL ANGONE

Designed by *ashton brye* for *Listen to Your Day: The Life-Changing Practice of Paying Attention.*

This sounds simple and straightforward, but believe you me, I know that with the craziness of the day, and two kids literally climbing your face while the other two complain about each other to you at the same time, talking to the person who you married and live with is not as easy as it once seemed.

During the infatuation stage, you sat for hours, gazing into each other's eyes and sharing one piece of spaghetti like the Lady and the Tramp you were.

Now, for many of us, it might feel like you could put one of those silver bar piercings through your nostrils and tattoo "Steve" on your forehead, and three days later your spouse would finally look at you, puzzled, and say, "What did you do to your face?"

I think one of the worst habits of marriage many of us fall into is that we simply stop looking at each other.

There are so many blaring, fighting, whining, lovable, dancing, singing, hugging, pooping, attention-demanding tasks running around the house all day who I swear are purposefully looking for new and opportune ways to seriously hurt themselves and the sibling they've convinced to come with them for this ride down the stairs on a pillowcase while holding the goldfish with a rusty metal shovel.

Then there's work. Making money. Accounting for how you spent that money. Cleaning the house, which with kids feels like trying to sweep up confetti in Times Square during New Year's Eve. There are your parents. Their parents. So many diapers, trips to Costco for more diapers, then another trip to Costco the same day because you came home with diapers, a five-pound bag of quinoa, sixteen cans of olives, and yet you forgot the wipes.

Then apparently there are old cast iron pipes under the cement floor in the basement laundry room of your 1950s house. So one day you walk into said laundry room and your utility sink is now magically filled to the brim with a disgusting waste bucket of food. (In case you were wondering, yes, this happened to us. Long story short: our kitchen sink pipes run down and under our laundry room, the utility sink tied in as our overflow. Needless to say a fun surprise to find your laundry room sink filled with food and then, even funnier, the $5,000 it would take to fix it! When guests tour our house, I take them to see our new pipes. Because if you're dropping that much on something in your house, you better at least get some eyeballs on it.)

Basically, grown-up life can feel like someone is grabbing your face every day and screaming at it from the moment you wake up until the moment you pass out in bed.

No wonder we're all escaping into our phones for some peace and quiet. Yet, that "escape" becomes counterproductive as you look at the perfect picture of your friend with her four kids in matching outfits skipping through wildflowers like they're the real-life reincarnation of *The Partridge Family* meets *The Sound of Music*.

So when I'm talking about paying attention to your spouse, I'm starting at the most base level we can here. I'm not talking about anything radical, like you need to go on some hot yoga marriage retreat together in Bali. I'm not talking about climbing Everest together. I'm talking about sitting your butts down on the couch at the same time and looking at each other in the eyes. (And not comparing the other person to the couch on which you sit. That's always a bad idea.)

Naomi and I were in a group of couples going through a marriage book together, and we had a wonderful couple, Rich and Shelly Howard of OneFamily, come in to talk to us about the importance of "CouchTime." Of setting aside at least fifteen minutes three to four times a week to sit together as a couple in a "nonconflict" zone to talk. They stressed the importance of this for your marriage, but also how important it was for your kids to see you talking to each other in a calm, intentional way.

Sitting down. Putting phones out of arm's reach. Looking each other in the eyes. Talking. Listening. Repeat.

If you feel like you're having trouble communicating in your relationship, or let's say you've complained that your partner hardly talks or doesn't share their feelings—is it a problem with them not talking? Or is it a problem that you don't show them you're listening?

Because if you're repeatedly giving someone the nonverbal message that you're not really listening when they talk, then they are going to talk less. So the focus should become how to take ownership of how you are paying your attention, which in turn, will help the person speak way more honestly and freely than you continually complaining to them that they won't open up.

This is Relationship 101. Yet, for anyone who's been through some years in your marriage, and brought some kids into the mix along the way, Relationship 101 can feel like it's getting wrapped up into last night's poopy diaper and thrown out in the trash.

Paying Attention to What Matters Most before Having a "Discussion"

When we do need to discuss somewhat weighty issues in our relationship, which happens to all of us, we'd be much more successful heading off runaway discussions that are speeding toward the cliff of a full-blown argument if we paid attention to the overarching goal of our relationship before bringing up the discussion.

When you are frustrated with your spouse or dating partner, the initial response can be to come out guns blazing in a conversation and demanding some kind of change. This will instantly leave the other person feeling ambushed and attacked, as they quickly hunker behind some rock to reload and go on the offensive themselves.

Instead of this course of action, what if we framed the conversation differently and made sure our attention stayed anchored in a more important place.

Instead of going on the attack, you tactfully usher in the conversation by grounding your reasons for bringing this up in your common goals as a couple. You say something like, "I love you and I know we both want to have a trusting, honest relationship where we discuss things with each other and build an even stronger relationship. So I wanted to discuss this with you . . ."

By framing an important discussion in this way, it helps you both pay attention to the ultimate goal instead of throwing hand grenades at each other and blowing apart the whole thing with every fight.

Framing the conversation first in common goals helps you both pay attention to what matters the most.

It's not an "I want to have a healthy relationship, but you're really pissing me off and screwing this up!" It's "I want to have a healthy relationship, I want to build a strong foundation, and this is why I want to discuss this with you, so that we can continue to build a strong foundation."

You see, you're keeping the focus on the common overarching goal. You're both paying attention to what really matters, so the discussions and details of this day will only strengthen that foundation instead of destroying it with every knockout battle between you two.

I think in relationships of all kinds—romance, business, and friendships—we'd be much better served looking at discussions through the lens of our common goals together instead of going on the attack. You present the discussion on a platter in between you two instead of just running up and throwing it in their face.

Listen to Your Relationships Today

We war for our marriages, usually not in some big, epic battle, but we war for our marriages in our small, daily decisions. We fight for our relationships by paying attention to them.

In marriage, you have to fight against all the things that want to keep you fighting. War for your marriage, not against it.
    —*101 Secrets for Your Twenties*

Issues with three Cs: Commitment. Communicating. Compatibility. How often would these blaring issues in marriage lose their jagged edge if every day we were getting together and polishing them down together on the couch. (That might've come off a little dirty, but hey, talking to each other and looking at each other in the eyes can lead to this again too! But that "conversation" might be best served after the kids go to sleep.)

> Do you think the people you love most feel like you pay attention to them?

We could go through study after study about our lack of focus and ability to concentrate on others. But I simply want to get to the heart of the day here with you, and me, with this one question.

Do you think the people you love most feel like you pay attention to them?

Not sure? Go ask them. I'll wait here. Yes, I realize I'm distracting you from this book, and that's okay. We should pay attention to the people we say we love, shouldn't we? So, do we?

Thoughts about Kids While Gardening

Then there's paying attention to our kids. In my house, it's like each kid is their own radio station, all playing songs from different genres, at the same time, at max volume. Yet, I really want to pay attention to what my kids are saying and doing. I know they are saying so much that I don't hear. And they have so much to teach me that I'm not paying attention to.

They are showing me their heart, their strengths, their values every day, and I fear I far too often miss it. Because I'm distracted. Because I'm overwhelmed. Because I'm selfish. What if I tuned my ears to the beautiful song they are singing. What if I truly paid attention to their petals that are blossoming right in front of my eyes.

What if I truly paid attention to the person they are and the person they are becoming, so that when times get rough and confusing and uncomfortable and ambiguous, I can help point them back home. I can be a compass of sorts that says, "I know who you are. You're beautiful, you're talented, you're smart, you're loving," all with real-life examples that I've seen over the years.

Shouldn't we pay the most attention to the things we say matter the most? How have we gotten this so bass ackwards, so to speak? Because far too often the things we pay so much attention to mean so very little in the important, grand scheme of things.

> **Because far too often the things we pay so much attention to mean so very little in the important, grand scheme of things.**

What is the cost of not properly paying attention to our kids? It's often said that kids who are acting up and misbehaving are simply trying to get their parents' attention, for better or worse.

Too many kids feel completely unseen and unheard.

How often do we spend time with our kids without paying any attention to them? Just the thought of this makes me want to cry. We spend so much time worrying about money, getting a bigger house, more clients, bigger Instagram followings, whatever it may be. But our kids don't really need or care about all that stuff. What they really need is you. Your love and attention. A parent who sees them, so they never feel like they're going at anything in life alone. I'm not talking about being God in their lives. I'm talking about being a reflection that points them back to a loving God when they feel alone.

ELEVEN

Stop, Pause, and Pay Attention—More on the Practice and Power of Paying Attention to People

Can you just stop what you're doing and listen?

We've all probably said this line and had this line said to us many times over the years. We say this to the person we're trying to talk to because we can tell by their delayed responses that they are caught up in some action and aren't hearing us. Or the words they are saying are not really matching up with what we just said, so we can pretty easily tell whether they are paying attention to us.

So we will either ask them to stop and listen, or more likely, we will just stop talking and move on because we've received the nonverbal cue that what we're saying is really not that important to them.

If it feels like your coworker who is writing an email while talking to you is only catching about half the things you're saying, it's most likely because they are.

If you find yourself getting frustrated at your spouse/partner because it feels like they're not actually listening as they look at their phone while you're talking and they're halfheartedly responding with words and phrases that don't match what you're saying... you're probably right. They're not really paying you any attention. Our brains cannot focus on two things at the exact same time.

We think we can multitask, but more and more studies are showing that we're not as good at multitasking as we think we are. We don't really do two or three tasks at once. Psychologists refer to this as the *switch cost*. We merely switch from task to task, with a cost of awareness, productivity, and comprehension each time we switch for each thing we are trying to "multitask" between.

So if someone is trying to have a conversation with you at work or at home, that should probably mean you need to intentionally stop what you're doing and look at them.

Unless they are the *Lingering Coworker* who won't stop coming in and talking so you are trying to give them the nonverbal cue to leave because you are busy. Just saying.

But if it is a conversation you need to have or a person you want to have a relationship with, if you simply stop what you're doing and look at them, right then and there, no matter the person's "love language," you've just shown them you actually care about them. You care about them more than what you were doing. That says a lot.

Now, for me, this can be extremely difficult. Let's say my family is throwing a dinner party at our house. It's hard to be the host and listen, isn't it? I want to make the party go smoothly, have the food cooked deliciously, and the like. But I become so focused on making all the details go smoothly that I'll catch myself even getting up and walking out of the room to check on something "important" while someone is in the middle of explaining something important to me.

Now, if the chicken is on fire in the oven, that might be a good time to run out. But if I just want to lower the music a touch, instead of just going over and turning it down while someone is talking to me, I could at least wait for the person to finish their sentence, then say, "I really want to hear what you're saying so I'm going to turn the music down." Then sitting back down, looking them in the eyes, and saying, "So you were saying that Timmy hit a home run! Tell me more . . ."

Right then I've verbally and nonverbally shown them that I care about them and what they're saying. And isn't the point of the dinner party to be that the person you invited over feels like you care about them and want to be their friend? Because no matter how good the shrimp scampi is or how perfectly placed that decoration was to set the tone of the evening, if you're continually walking out on someone while they talk, the message will be loud and clear, and it probably isn't the message you were hoping to convey.

I wonder if part of the draw of visiting a therapist or counselor is the fact that they are paying undivided attention to us. Sure, we are paying them to pay attention. Sure, they are actively taking notes about how screwed up we are, but heck, we'll take it!

Paying attention to someone is the foundation of connection. It seems simple, yet many of us need to intentionally work on forming this new habit daily.

Stop. Pause. Pay them your attention. See if your relationships begin to change.

The Physical Components of Paying and Showing Attention

Once we've paused and are paying attention, what are some other ways we can do a better job of showing attention and paying attention, all in one? What are some other ways we can start building habits of *showing* attention, which then in turn, helps us *pay* attention—whether at home, work, in the coffee shop, wherever?

In Your Eyes

In 1989, during two studies, strangers who looked at each other's eyes, unbroken, for two minutes reported increased feelings of passionate love for each other.[1]

In *Psychology Today*, science journalist Lydia Denworth explains that "eye contact activates the social brain, the neural regions that orchestrate our responses to other people. Making eye contact signals to another person that you are paying attention. It is one way we share intention and emotion, and it requires that you synchronize eye movements with someone else."[2]

Eyes are powerful. So much so that you can even feel someone looking at you from across a crowded coffee shop, right? You've probably experienced countless moments like this. You look up, and it's a friend you haven't seen in a while who was staring at you to, what, get your attention? You're with friends in a dark, deafening club, yet you can still feel someone's eyes on you from across the room. Eyes are powerful instruments for showing and paying attention.

Making sustained eye contact is literally the simplest way you tell someone that you are paying attention to them. And at the same time, tell your brain, "Hey, up there. You really need to listen to them!"

Simply looking someone in the eyes as they talk will tell them you care about them more than any words that you say.

Shifting eyes, wandering eyes, eyes that continually look at your phone or watch are telling the person across from you that they're not that important. Your eyes are nonverbally showing them your level of focus and attention. We can all probably think of a time that the person we were talking to kept looking over our shoulder at something else so often that we've completely lost track of what we were talking about and now we're looking too: "What are you looking at?"

Even if that's not your intention, eye contact is the portal to your perceived attention.

This is why you'll also see parents instinctively or intentionally kneel down when a child is pleading their heart out so that the parent can get at their eye level, which shows the child, "I'm here for you and I'm listening."

Eye Contact and Anxiety

This eye contact might be harder for some who have a certain anxiety or fear come over them when looking someone in the eyes. Some people experience a social anxiety disorder and have to work through the fear and anxiety of looking at someone in the eyes. People can work on overcoming this anxiety through cognitive behavioral therapy and the like, but I know personally I can struggle with this as well at times.

I was a very shy kid, and both my parents were highly recognizable figures at a large organization where I also went to school—aka, I grew up as a pastor's kid. I spent more time in that building than I did at my own house.

Everywhere I went, people knew me and wanted to talk to me. I really, honestly didn't want to talk to them. I felt nervous and wanted to escape. So over the years I've really had to intentionally work on being comfortable looking people in the eyes and talking. Sometimes, when I start feeling anxious, I'll even do a little trick of taking my glasses off during a conversation just so their eyes are a little bit blurry. This helps me not feel so nervous with their white orbs staring into my soul!

I want to show people I care about them, but if I keep looking somewhere else, I'm showing them that I'm not paying attention. Now I'm not talking about staring without blinking or never shifting your gaze anywhere else. Because that might freak anyone and everyone out.

But give someone your eye contact and they will give you their attention in return. Attention in conversation, looking at each other, is a handshake agreement between two people, subconsciously telling the other, "Hey, I'm in this with you! Let's really talk!"

Body Position and Paying Attention

What are some other physical components to paying attention to others?

Leaning forward in your chair while having coffee with someone will subconsciously tell your mind to pay attention. It will also subconsciously tell the other person that you are listening, which will help them speak more freely. Then they will most likely start leaning forward as well, matching your body position as the conversation flows between both parties actively being participants in the conversation at hand.

Treat your body position like you have an arrow going straight out from your navel, aimed directly at the person you're talking with. The closer someone is to the direct path of that arrow, the more they will feel important to you in that conversation. The more that arrow is pointing away or shifting away from that person, the less they will feel you are paying attention to them. Geometry and angles play a big role in paying attention.

When we lean back in our chair or have our arms crossed in front of us, we are guarding ourselves and giving off the impression that we want to leave the conversation or are uninterested.

As I'm writing this in a coffee shop, I literally just watched a person give attention by changing his body position. He was talking to someone across from him with both chairs set at angles, with a table in the middle. One person in the conversation grabbed the edges of his chair and shifted it so that his shoulders, stomach, and knees, were all pointed directly at the person across from him. As he did this, I saw the conversation become livelier and more animated. He made a nonverbal investment in the conversation and laid down a payment of attention.

Go to a busy coffee shop or restaurant where people like to sit, and observe the conversations in the room. Count which conversations you think are going well and which are going poorly.

After you've counted, go back and pay attention to their body positions. I'm guessing that with most of the conversations you've viewed as going well, the people involved in them are both leaning forward.

Smiles and Head Nods

In those conversations that are going well, there's probably also a natural flow of smiling taking place with the people talking and head nodding. Smiling is a big nonverbal cue that you're paying attention to someone and are into what they are saying. The person across from you will have much stronger feelings toward you and will start smiling in return. Now you're both feeling that this is going well, and you like each other. Trust and affinity are being built just by simple smiles and head nods, which say, "I hear you and I agree."

But, please don't smirk! A smirk is a smile typically without teeth where one side of your lips is going higher than the other. Smiles are more symmetrical, smirks are not. We like symmetrical! In design, in facial construction, and in our smiles!

Smirkers have the opposite effect in conversations. Maybe you're not even intending this message to come across, but a smirk connotes smugness or sarcasm. You're implying that the person across from you doesn't know what they are talking about and that you know better. A consistent smirk shatters trust and affinity.

Again, I know this is not rocket science and you've heard some of these things before. However, as face-to-face conversations and paying attention to each other becomes a lost art form, these simple techniques that you can learn and practice become both the science and art of good conversations. Not just good conversations unto themselves, but you're conveying the message before you even open your mouth that you care for the person sitting across from you.

125

Paying attention
to someone is
the foundation of
connection...
Stop.
Pause.
Pay them your attention.
See if your relationships
begin to change.
    - Paul Angone

DESIGNED BY CHRISTIAN_CALLIGRAPHY_ FOR *LISTEN TO YOUR DAY*

And if there's a conversation that you don't feel is going well, then by looking in their eyes, smiling, leaning forward, facing them directly, nodding your head, all these simple nonverbal cues can transform the conversation in front of you. You have the power to tell this person they are important, which in turn, will help them have more positive feelings toward you.

Now, When We Open Our Mouths

Obviously it won't be much of a conversation if your mouths don't open and words don't start coming out. When they do, what can you say to help you pay more attention and show that you're paying attention?

Let's start here: don't be the "Me Monster" like comedian Brian Regan so aptly and hilariously describes in one of his bits about being at a dinner party: "One guy talking plenty for everybody . . . Me, myself, right? And then I. And then myself. Me, me! I couldn't tell this one about I because I was talking about myself. And then . . . me. Me. ME!"[3]

Someone you consider a good person to talk to is probably one who shows a genuine interest in you. I was going to a chiropractor for a while who was such a good conversationalist. He was adjusting my body, which made me feel better. But even more than that, he also just made me feel good about myself. So much so, that I started paying attention to how he was accomplishing that.

First, he was really good at remembering things I talked about on earlier visits, and he'd ask me how those were going now. He'd probably seen a couple hundred patients between my visits, and he would still bring up specific details from our previous conversations. I'm not going to lie, he made me feel special. I genuinely liked talking to him, because he showed interest in me and just let me talk about myself!

I was so impressed with his ability, I asked one day if he took notes in his system after each visit about what his patients talked about. He just kind of laughed and replied, "No, I just genuinely care about my patients and want them to feel that."

Job well done, sir. It definitely showed. I think I kept going to the chiropractor about two months longer than I would have because I liked talking to him so much. It was like an encouraging counseling session, whilst also getting my neck cracked. A truly immersive therapy experience!

I would say for most of us, we don't innately have this skill of a strong memory and genuine curiosity in others. I'll raise my hand here. I'm a keynote speaker and author, so I love telling stories and talking about myself. I have to work on the skill of showing interest in others. I care about others. I'm just not always the best at showing it. I'm passionate about what I do, and I love talking about it. But I know this isn't the best recipe for relationship building and making a connection.

So instead of parachuting in and holding everyone hostage to the latest stories about how amazing you are, I encourage you to focus on the first five minutes of the conversation and try not to talk about yourself at all. Make it a personal challenge or a game.

Ask the other person questions about themselves. If you've talked to this person before, ask them about things they've told you in the past. Already, you're showing that you care and you were paying attention so well that you actually remember things about them. Big win!

You could meet someone for the first time, not talk about yourself at all, and instead just ask the person one good question after another. They will leave the conversation and tell their friend, "Hey, I just met them and I really like 'em," without even realizing that you didn't say one thing about yourself.

In the next five conversations you have, try implementing "The First Five Minutes" and build this skill of asking a person questions without saying anything about yourself for the first five minutes of a conversation.

We hear stories and anecdotes that former president Bill Clinton would be in a crowded party and showed such interest in someone else that it would make them feel like they were the only person in the room. Now, whether that was genuine interest or a mastered skill by a master politician, I'll leave that up for debate.

Mr. Fred Rogers was described the same way. He had a gift of truly seeing people, no matter if they were a young child in a wheelchair or the president of the United States. I think Mr. Rogers summed up his

> We show and give love by showing and giving our attention.

"why" behind his skill to make others feel heard: "The world needs a sense of worth, and it will achieve it only by its people feeling that they are worthwhile."[4]

I wish I could say I possess the same skill. People are a pretty consistent and important part of our day. We must pay attention to them.

We show and give love by showing and giving our attention.

Pay Attention to Your Relationship Status

Now for a quick macro view of the relationships in your life. I used to definitely be a "Friends Are Friends Forever" kind of person. Then I'd feel very sad and let down whenever certain relationships faded away.

The older I've gotten, the more I've realized, and become at peace with, the fact that certain relationships in your life are for a certain season. Some relationships continue through life, some don't. That's normal and that's okay.

I think we need to stop feeling guilty or surprised by the fact that not all friendships last forever. Continually clinging to certain relationships that are no longer healthy in the season you're in can become problematic. Letting go of relationships that you need to release can be an important part of growth, change, and cultivating healthy relationships in the days you're now living.

I'm not saying get rid of all past friendships. What I'm saying is that if you're not doing life with those people anymore (a new job, graduation, life-stage changes with marriage or kids, etc.), then naturally the connection and the importance of that relationship for both parties will change.

For example, if you're newly married and trying to hold on to all the same patterns, places, and people you hung out with in your single days that's going to become a problem.

If you're still hanging out with your "ex" because, *hey, we're still good friends*, but your current partner is none too keen to see this relationship continue, you need to pay attention to what this relationship really means to you. Should you be getting emotional or mental support from a past relationship when obviously, at some point, it's going to cause a huge rift in your current one?

Parents and children walk this line together in many different ways. Hopefully, the child-parent relationship will be a through-life relationship that's going to be in your life forever. But the importance and weight of that relationship need to change to be healthy and functional.

If your child is forty years old and you're treating him or her like they're thirteen, running to their rescue whenever there are issues, that's where you all start riding around on a fun little carousel of enabling. The "grown-up child" keeps riding that same horse, even though it doesn't go up and down anymore because it wasn't meant for a 200-pound adult. The ride is broken, yet everyone involved keeps paying their quarters to perpetuate something that needs to be fixed.

If you're newly married, having arguments with your spouse, and then leaving and sleeping at your parents' house while sharing all your marital problems with your mom, that's not healthy either.

At some point, parents should no longer have full control and say over their kids' lives. And kids should no longer be depending on their parents to meet their needs and solve their problems. The parent-child relationship is a constantly growing and changing dynamic that will look different in different seasons. That's normal and healthy.

We need to pay attention to the current status of our different relationships. Are we still trying to cling to the way that relationship was and the function it held in the past when we're no longer living in that same season?

Yes, some friends will stay friends forever. But those friendships too will naturally have different shades and colors as life goes on.

You can hold on to a false belief that "I'm never going to change." But that's not the badge of honor you may think it is. That's continually holding on to the scraps of the past when there's a full banquet of new experiences and growth waiting in front of you. There are core values and beliefs that might stay ingrained in who you are and how you want to live your life. That's important. Yet, I believe we all should be changing by becoming more of who we are created to be.

You change. Relationships change. But our ability to give love by giving people our attention shouldn't. Are you loving people well in your conversations? Are you showing them attention? Whether a spouse, child, parent, colleague, manager, or client, the health and success of that relationship will ultimately come down to whether or not that person feels paid attention to by you.

No investment in a relationship is more important than the payment of your attention.

PRACTICE THE FIRST FIVE MINUTES

In your next meeting with someone, try to implement the First Five Minutes, where you ask them questions and try not to talk about yourself. Then after the conversation is over, write down what you remember about what they said. Doesn't have to be long and drawn out. Just take a few notes afterward. Writing down what they said when the conversation is over is a good strategy to help you start building the habit of listening to what they're saying. If you get to the end, and you can't remember one thing they talked about, were you actually listening?

PRACTICE PAYING ATTENTION
TO YOUR RELATIONSHIPS

Write down your top three relationships. How much attention do you give them on a daily basis? Write down one action you can take this week to pay more attention to each of them.

PART 2

CULTIVATING MINDSET MODELS

Have you ever thought to yourself, *I wish I thought like they do!*
Now is your chance. For these next few chapters, we will be working on paying attention to our days in different ways through various mindset models. These mindset models are powerful tools to change the way we think and pay attention to what our day is telling us. I'm going to present different mindset models for you to view your day through, then we're going to write down what we discover. I promise you're going to notice profound things that you've never seen before. You're going to spot moonwalking bears.

These mindset models are amazing ways to unlock your view. Some might come more naturally to you, and some might feel completely unorthodox. That's normal. Basically these are methods for practicing new ways of paying attention. We can talk about the importance of paying attention. We can talk study after study about distraction, mindfulness, and the like. But we want action.

We want revelation and new ideas. We want to be more present in our day and paying attention to what is important.

I don't want to give you the answers from my life. I want to help you see all the answers in yours. I want you to peel back the ingredients of your signature sauce—that flavor and substance you bring to the world that no one else can. I first wrote about some of these mindset models in *101 Questions You Need to Ask in Your Twenties (And Let's Be Honest, Your Thirties Too)*, but now I want to expand on these and take them much further.

These mindset models are training and practice for paying attention in different ways.

Let's say there's a gigantic maple tree that's been sitting in your backyard for seventy years. You see the tree there every day, but do you actually *see* it? It's so amazing, this ultimate pillar of life you have in your own yard, yet you miss so much about it every day.

These mindset models are ways of looking at the tree through different focuses and lenses. One day you focus on just the leaves. You study them up close. You see all the amazing, intricate veins running through the leaf to give it structure and nutrients. Another day you notice the bark. Another day you try to figure out how tall it really is. The next day you study all the animals that come and go from the tree in a day. Then one day you look closer for all the bugs. Another day you try studying the roots and figure out how far out they go.

After looking at this tree and studying it, you begin to have a fuller, richer appreciation. You see things about it that you never did before. You realize the amazing ecosystem the tree is unto itself. You finally see something for the magical creation it is, and it has been staring you in the face every day.

Same with these mindset models. They help us see the amazing, magical things all around us that we weren't able to see before. Sure, there might be crossover between various models, as each might incorporate a little of the other. But each model encourages us to see our day in a different way, giving us various lenses to radically change the way we pay attention.

Let's take a look.

TWELVE

Entrepreneur
Mindset Model

Seeing problems not as obstacles but
opportunities for us to create a solution.
A problem is the pathway to a purposeful plan.

If we tried to think of a good idea, we wouldn't have been
able to think of a good idea. You just have to find the solution for a problem in your own life.

—Brian Chesky, cofounder of Airbnb

Entrepreneurs have become the rock stars of the twenty-first cen-
tury, living/embodying the American dream—to work when, how,
where, and on whatever they want. Young, hardworking employees
leaving well-paid jobs at some of the most iconic places in the
nation to go join a five-person team in the Bay Area, in some

downtown factory that used to make cast-iron anchors, to revolutionize the way cats sleep.

An entrepreneur's ultimate goal is to create a unicorn—a company with a billion-dollar valuation. Unicorn is a perfect description for how I've viewed entrepreneurs over the years. These mythical creatures that seemingly sleep four hours a day and bust out business plans for their angel investors like I bust out excuses for why I cannot get up before 8:00 a.m.

But at the heart, what if entrepreneurs are not that different than you and me? Maybe their main strength is that they pay attention in a different way than we do. Entrepreneurs simply see and lean into something that most of us complain about and avoid.

Entrepreneurs and Their Problems

For most of us, a problem is a problem. Something to be avoided. Something to complain about to others.

Entrepreneurs pay attention to their problems. Not only do they pay attention to them, they get ecstatic about them. When entrepreneurs see a problem, they see a business opportunity.

For entrepreneurs, a problem is the pathway to a plan. It is the pathway to a product. Ultimately, it is the pathway to profit.

Every business opportunity starts with a problem that needs to be solved. Entrepreneurs see questions that need answers and needs that are waiting to be met.

A problem we might avoid, an entrepreneur might embrace with loving arms and invite it home for tea so they might ask it a few questions. They don't run from a problem; they ask it to make itself at home and stay awhile.

Take, for example, Aaron Krause, a professional car detailer. One day, Aaron was waxing a car and then realized his worst fear–he scratched the car with the cleaning products he was using. But instead of kicking himself for the mistake, he paid attention to the problem. Why, as a professional car detailer, were the products offered to him damaging cars? This shouldn't happen.

So while developing his own line of products, Aaron began working on creating a new kind of sponge to solve the problem he experienced. After inventing it, he was able to get 3M to buy the business, with his buffing and polishing pads, but they left him the sponges because they had their own line. Aaron ended up boxing all his sponges and throwing them in storage.

Five years go by until Aaron was doing some spring cleaning and stumbled across his long-lost dream sitting next to that tub of old wires and connections we all hold on to, you know, just in case technology goes back fifteen years and these things become relevant again.

After dinner, his wife asked him to do the dishes. Aaron remembered his boxes of sponges and decided to try them out on the pots and pans that night. When faced with the new problem of the black gunk on the bottom of the pan, Aaron realized how effective his sponges were. He also noticed that the sponge became softer in hot water and hard in cold water.

Right then, Aaron felt he was on a million-dollar idea and he created Scrub Daddy.[1]

In 2012, after getting the product in a few local grocery stores and on QVC, Aaron was able to get on the show *Shark Tank*, where investor Lori Greiner made the investment of $200,000 for 20 percent of the company. What some of the sharks ridiculed as a high-priced novelty item (selling for a whole $2) that would never sell on the shelves now has a whopping $209 million dollar valuation as of 2019 and was featured on *20/20*, with the show lauding it as "Shark Tank's most successful product to date."[2]

If you think successfully finding an investor on a TV show is the only way to make it work, cue Jamie Siminoff. Jamie was attempting to launch a gardening start-up, so like most fabled entrepreneurs, his office and company workshop was his garage. While working from his garage, Jamie started experiencing a daily problem. He couldn't hear the doorbell. Important packages were being delivered, but Jamie was missing signing off and receiving them.

Jamie went looking for a solution. He started by searching for a product that he could connect to his smartphone to see who was at the door, but he couldn't find anything.

(Sidenote: If you go looking for a product to solve your problem and you're sure there must be something already out there, yet one doesn't exist, that's a good sign you're onto something.)

So Jamie created a Wi-Fi–enabled camera doorbell. When he installed it at his own home and his wife told him that the camera made her feel safer, he knew he was onto something possibly bigger than the gardening start-up was ever going to be. Thus, the initial creation of the product DoorBot.

Pouring all his money, and then a lot more money he didn't have, into the company, Jamie was able to get on *Shark Tank* as his last-ditch effort to get himself out of debt and get DoorBot off the ground.

Jamie went on *Shark Tank* with DoorBot, and yet he left a failure. He was unsuccessful in convincing the Sharks to make an investment.

Yet, only five years later, with the product renamed the Ring doorbell, Jamie sold his company to Amazon for over one billion dollars. And then the real kicker, he appeared again on *Shark Tank*, but this time as an investor.[3]

Beta Testing

When finding solutions to these problems, entrepreneurs are all about the beta test. Version 1.0, 1.7, 2.1, 3.9, 59.1 . . . entrepreneurs keep the beta-testing party going for as long as they can, inviting anyone over with a checkbook to hear them talk about their latest solution to the problem that is not quite the final solution yet.

When beta testing, basically what entrepreneurs are doing is creating strategic and purposeful failures. They plan to fail. That's the point of the beta test. They don't conceal the solution until they know it doesn't have any flaws. Because they know that's unrealistic. Perfection will never happen in the lab. They need to beta test solutions to the problem so the flaws can be uncovered quicker and with more efficiency.

The Method of an Entrepreneur

All right, you might be thinking, *What's the point of all this talk about entrepreneurs and paying attention to my day?* Especially if you have zero desire to ever start a business from your garage where seemingly all great entrepreneurial stories originate.

First, you might be more entrepreneur than you think. We're all starting something. We're all creating something. We're all coming up with solutions in our life, our house, our family, our work. Sure, you might not be creating a business around it, but that doesn't mean you're not entrepreneurial.

Heck, I left my steady salary job in 2013 to go full-time on my own as an author and keynote speaker. And it was around five years into it that I even started throwing around the title of *entrepreneur*. Again, I thought entrepreneurs were mythical unicorns starting billion-dollar ideas out of their garage. I've never written a page in my garage. It's small, cold, and smells like . . . a garage.

Yet, I was creating a business out of my books, keynote talks, and all the research I'd done through my master's in organizational leadership. I created my website **allgroanup.com** to reach readers; **paulangone.com** to showcase my college and corporate speaking; an online course at **signaturesauce.com** to help people on a deeper level; and the *All Groan Up* podcast. Basically I was creating all these things around my business but never considered myself an entrepreneur while doing it.

But even more importantly, at the heart of the whole thing was a huge need and problem. I really struggled after college finding my way. I had so many big life questions. I didn't feel like a kid, yet I didn't quite feel like an adult. I still felt like I was playing house; my dad's coat and tie still felt like they were hanging off me. How do you figure out all these big life answers to your career, relationships, identity, faith, purpose, and meaning when you don't even feel like you're asking the right questions?

So I started writing about the problem. I knew other twentysomethings were going through similar issues when I started being a sounding board for others. Because I couldn't find books that I felt spoke to this ambiguous season of life, I started writing one. It was part therapeutic, part strategic to hopefully turn it into a book and speaking career someday. Yet, at the heart was this huge need I felt was there but not being met. At the heart was the pain and confusion I knew people were going through that was leading to anxiety, depression, and hopelessness.

It was the problem that kept me going. Through years of rejection and rewrites, every publisher turned me down because I didn't have a platform, and some told me there wasn't a place for books for twentysomethings. Authors wrote to kids, young adults, or adults—that's it. There was no space in the industry for ambiguity.

Yet, I knew the publishers were wrong. I'd stared at the problem face-to-face for years. I'd felt the struggle and frustration all too clearly. And knew so many in my same situation.

It took me eight years from writing that first page to seeing my first book published. The story is a long one, with the final tipping point being a blog post I wrote called "21 Secrets for Your 20s" on my website allgroanup.com that went viral on Pinterest, of all places. But after all the dreams of bestselling books and speaking tours had faded away, it was the need for the book that kept me going. It was the vision of people standing on the ledge, losing hope, who would someday need me standing there next to them. Telling them there is hope and encouraging them to take a step back.

It was a question I kept asking myself, and now ask others, that kept me going: "Who will I not be able to help if I give up now?"

It was how starkly I saw and felt the problem and need that kept me going.

What's Your Problem?

Today, I want you to look at your day like an entrepreneur. I don't want you to avoid your problems, I want you to pay close attention to them. I want you to grab them by the ears and stare them in their eyes.

Not sure you'll be able to recognize them? Well, what do you find yourself complaining about? What do you find yourself frustrated with? Many books will tell you not to focus on the burdens of your day, just count your blessings. Like I've written about before, I'm all for paying attention to the countless ways we each are blessed.

But today I want you to think like an entrepreneur and get excited about your problems! Look for what bothers you. Look for what aggravates you. Maybe you even need to recognize your own physical, mental, or emotional pain.

You see, passion often comes from pain. Passion can be birthed out of a huge problem that you know all too well. It's hard to be passionate about something you've never gone through yourself.

Personal experience with a problem births passion to help you, and others, overcome.

Pay attention to your problems.

Is it inefficiencies with the way things are done at home or in the office? Is it the pain you see in certain types of people because you've experienced that same pain yourself? Is there a product that you use every day that annoys you, but you've just never recognized it before? Like looking at the smelly, disgusting sponges we all use every day without thinking about them. Aaron Krause looked at them and saw a better way. He saw the problem and he leaned into finding a solution, giving us Scrub Daddy.

Pay attention to your problems. Yet, don't see them as problems to then be avoided. See them as these golden opportunities for you to create a solution. How can you come up with solutions for yourself and others if you first don't see and understand the problem?

If we don't have problems that we're intentionally paying attention to, our minds will not be able to find solutions.

If we have the "it's all good" mentality where we pretend we have no problems, in reality we're just avoiding all of them behind our fake smiles. Instead of hiding in the dark, saying "it's all good" as we rock back and forth, afraid of everything lurking out there, we face our problems and pain head-on, and we turn on the light. We're illuminating the reality around us so that we can then tackle the challenges in front of us.

There's a joy like no other in overcoming problems, pains, and challenges. Blinding ourselves from our problems does not make them go away. Paying attention to them, then coming up with solutions, is a gift of fulfillment and purpose. Artificially keeping yourself in the dark because you're afraid of what the light might reveal is a hard way to progress through life.

Yet, many of us aren't hiding from the problems around us. We see problems—maybe too many of them. But we never shift to creating solutions to them. We get stuck in the crappy. We complain about them. We run from them and resent them. We passively see the problem and feel powerless to do anything about it.

But the moment we start working toward a "better way" is the moment we start living a better day. Sorry, I was apparently channeling my inner infomercial when I wrote that previous sentence. It would probably be better used describing a magic mop or cheese grater that will also iron your clothes. How about the moment we start working toward a "better way" is the moment our brain becomes alive in a different way?

Now you're going throughout your day looking for ways to solve that problem. Ideas are hitting you when you're showering. Aha moments are happening more readily, because you have a problem that needs you to find a solution.

Your brain likes a challenge.

I think all of us are looking for purpose. Look to your problems as the compost where life can grow. You'll find that rich and decadent purpose can come when you start working that soil. Then who knows where the solution will take you. Not just waking up with more excitement or tackling a project with more resolve. Maybe it's a billion-dollar business like Jamie Siminoff because he got sick of missing the doorbell while working away in his garage.

Maybe it's a book or piece of art, speaking to a struggle and issue you know all too well.

> **Your brain likes a challenge.**

Maybe solving a problem leads to a new role in your current job and even a promotion.

But don't worry too much about the outcome of solving the problem just yet. Chances are the outcome will look nothing like you expect, sitting here right now. We can see only so far. The path, the time, and the result will look very different.

As I wrote before while in my bathtub, the best things in your life, 99.99 percent won't happen at the time, in the place, or in the way you expected. So the next time things don't go as planned . . . that's probably the exact plan after all.

Don't get stuck on finding the perfect solution. Just start tinkering away at it. Start beta testing. Start experimenting. Don't feel like you need to know the solution right now where you sit. Too many of us become overwhelmed with taking that first step. Just baby-step it.

Beta test your day. Try something new to solve your problem, knowing that it's not supposed to work. It's supposed to fail. But understand that's the only way you can know what you currently don't know.

Start paying attention to your problems. Then watch as solutions and answers begin to reveal themselves to you. Then beta test and tinker. Entrepreneurs are not mythical unicorns; they simply see and solve problems. *We employ the* **Entrepreneur Mindset Model** *by seeing problems not as obstacles but opportunities for us to create a solution. A problem is the pathway to a purposeful plan.* Focus the next few days on filling out the Entrepreneurial Mindset Model below. Write down any and all problems you see throughout the day. Something you're struggling with personally. Something that frustrates you or that you find yourself complaining about. Big or small. Don't edit whether the problem is worth noting or not. Just write it down.

Then start thinking through possible ways to solve this problem. Brainstorm ideas as you go about your day. Again don't edit based on whether you think the solution will work or not.

That's what the beta-testing section is about. Start brainstorming ways so you can begin experimenting with a solution. Again, beta testing is all about failing quickly. You're not going to solve a problem with your first go.

Fail, tweak, then try again. Failure is a great clarifier.

The **ENTREPRENEUR MINDSET MODEL** sees problems not as obstacles but opportunities for us to create a solution. A problem is the pathway to a purposeful plan.

Entrepreneur Mindset Model

Problem	Solutions	Beta Testing

Problem	Solutions	Beta Testing

THIRTEEN

Farmer Mindset Model

Paying attention to the time and season
that decisions need to be made, all with
the "health of the whole" in mind.

Complete your work outside,
and get your fields ready for next season;
after that's done, build your house.

—Proverbs 24:27

Farmers know the seasons. Their whole livelihood is built on taking the proper action in the proper season. They deeply comprehend the cycle of life for which they live and work.

Farmers also understand that their whole livelihood begins with the soil. Life starts with the health of the soil, and all living things go back into the ecosystem of the soil. If the soil is stripped, if it is leeched, if it is never replenished with nutrients, then it can no longer produce.

There's a big difference between rich soil and dry dirt. The health of the soil can be the difference between a rich, productive ecosystem full of trillions of living organisms or the Dust Bowl.

Practicing the **Farmer Mindset Model** means *paying attention to the time and season that decisions need to be made, all with the "health of the whole" in mind.*

How you feed your soil and make the right calls in the right season comes down to making the right decision at the right time. A decision is only as effective as the season for which it exists. Proverbs warns us about the consequences:

> Once I passed by the property of a slacker,
>   by the vineyard of a foolish man.
> You should have seen it! The entire field was overgrown
>   with thorns.
> Every inch was covered with weeds.
> Even the stone wall was crumbling down.
> I took a moment to take it all in.
>   The scene taught me:
> "A little sleep, a little rest,
>   a few more minutes, a nice little nap."
> But soon poverty will be on top of you like a robber,
>   need will strike you down like a well-armed warrior.
>   Proverbs 24:30–34

We have to pay attention to the hard decisions and choices we know we need to make and the seasons we need to make them in. You can make the decision to pick a tomato after the first frost or you can pick it the week before. It's the same act. But the timing of that decision makes all the difference in the world between you throwing that tomato in a salad for the family or throwing it in the trash. Making the decision to pick the tomato at the right or wrong time changes how effective the outcome is.

147

The Seasons for Decisions

We all have different seasons in life and decisions we're possibly struggling to make. You know those decisions—you can't seem to escape from them. Where they're in your gut, spinning in circles like a baby practicing for delivery (and making you nauseous in the process).

You're facing a hard decision and find yourself at a crossroads with a choice to make. And you know that if you make the tough decision, the immediate path afterward is going to be extremely rocky, yet you absolutely know it's the right one. It's the path you need to take, even if on "paper" it's perceived as the wrong choice. Even if it's making you feel like a complete failure. I know those kinds of decisions all too well.

My senior year of college, I quit baseball. I gave up my scholarship and walked away from the sport that was my entire life. I felt like a failure, in a way. Quitting my senior year was never how I envisioned my baseball career to end. Yet, I knew deep in my spirit it was the decision I needed to make. My mind, body, and soul were telling me that baseball was over. I didn't quite know why, or what lay ahead, but I knew I needed to let it go.

A few months later, I was asked to emcee the biggest event at my college with my favorite professor, Dr. Greg Spencer. Committing to this was going to take months of preparation before getting up onstage in front of a thousand people at the Santa Barbara Bowl. Now that I had quit baseball, I had the time to say yes.

Being emcee that night was one of those seminal memories in my life that revealed so much to me about what I wanted to do in my future. Be onstage. Entertain. Speak. Create funny and engaging content. Inspire people and make them laugh.

Then, while I was emceeing the event, the director of college admissions, Joyce Luy, was in the audience and told herself she needed to hire me to work as an admissions counselor for Westmont College after graduation, which is exactly what I did.

A year into the job, my coworker came into my office and showed me the picture of an admissions counselor at a competing university, Azusa Pacific, and asked me if I had met her yet, because he thought she was attractive. Taking one look at the picture, I could see why. She was gorgeous, and no, I'd never met her.

A month later, I was sitting in a high school cafeteria in San Diego, helping judge a senior event, when the doors parted and it was like a spotlight from heaven pointed directly on the admissions counselor from Azusa Pacific who was just arriving.

I literally had an out-of-body experience, as I was out of my chair and walking toward her before I even knew what I was doing. I'm shy in social settings and was still fighting those insecurities of the acne-ridden high schooler I still felt like sometimes. Yet, here was this woman whom my friend just showed me a picture of, walking into a high school cafeteria late with all eyes on her, sunlight flooding in behind her through the opening doors. It was a scene fit for a romantic comedy.

So I walked right up to her, shook her hand, introduced myself, smiled, tried to say something funny and ask her a question, then I got the heck out of there before I could screw it up too much.

Little did I know why she had shown up at the very end of the event. She had just made an extremely hard decision herself. She officially broke up with her long-distance boyfriend the night before. It was a hard decision and she had been crying all morning, totally forgetting about the event that she was now extremely late for.

But when breaking up with her boyfriend, she knew that she knew it was the right thing to do. So much so, that when they were doing the breakup back and forth, she even told him she was breaking up with him because she knew she was going to meet her husband that summer and it wasn't him.

Cue me walking straight to her like a magnet just doing what it was designed to do. After telling her ex what she said, she was definitely paying attention too.

Now nearly fourteen years of marriage and four kids later, I literally love, adore, trust, and appreciate this woman more and more every year. What would've happened if I would've just held on to that last year of baseball, gritting it out because I'm not a quitter? What if my wife Naomi hadn't broken up with her boyfriend the night before we met because she so deeply knew that God had something different in store for her?

I feel so extremely blessed when I look at my marriage and kids, and it literally makes me feel nauseous to even ask the what-ifs. What if neither of us would've made those hard decisions that we could have easily not made? How wildly different would our lives be right now?

But sometimes those tough decisions are not to leave something—sometimes those hard decisions are to stay. That is the hardest decision to make. To stay in the job you don't necessarily love because you need to learn some important skills before you go. To stay in the relationship because "the grass is always greener on the other side until you get there and realize it's because of all the manure."[1]

Sometimes the hard decision is to grow where you are instead of constantly pulling up your roots.

We must pay attention to the hard decisions we need to make. We must pay attention to what we know, deep down, is right. It might not even be necessarily what we want, as our emotions are all spinning and flipping inside us like a big wave has knocked us completely off our equilibrium.

We must plant our feet and pay attention to the season we're in. Is it time to sow or time to plant? Time to run to or time to run from? Time to end something or time to begin?

Actively Avoiding

Yet, for many of us, our first response to a hard decision we need to make is avoidance. We don't want to look like a failure, an embarrassment, or a fool. We don't want to admit if we mess up. We don't want to say that we have a problem.

But the real problem is that the decision does not just go away if we don't make it. It circles back and continues to slam into us. Like standing on a bumper car track holding a bowl full of chili and trying not to spill it all over yourself. Everything continually becomes a greater mess when we don't simply leave the place we know we're not supposed to be in. It all depends on the season of life you are in.

The hard decision that you know you need to make might be to forgive. It might be to release the pain, anger, and bitterness you've been chewing on for far too long. The acid is building up in your stomach and making you sick. You need to let the pain and anger go, as it's wrecking your body.

Another hard decision might be to ask for help. Maybe you've been trying to do something on your own for far too long, and the weight of it all is crushing you. Maybe you need to seek help because the crutch you've been using to keep you upright is splintering and you keep finding yourself falling face-first on the ground. Sometimes the hard decision is knowing that you need help.

Paying Attention to the Connected and the Whole

Take John and Molly Chester, who left their LA apartment life to create a 214-acre thriving ecosystem with microorganisms, ground crops, animals, prey and predators, fruit trees, and crops, all working in unison together to create a full-bodied ecosystem working as it's supposed to. With death supporting life. Sure, the Chesters had some help with some (serious) investors and traditional farming experts like Alan York as they created Apricot Lane Farms, the main focus of their documentary film *The Biggest Little Farm*, but what they were able to accomplish is still admirable and astonishing.

With every new problem that popped up I'd first take a step back and watch it. Observation followed by creativity is becoming our greatest ally.[2]

—John Chester

As you watch the film, you realize that their secret power to success and only chance of survival was paying attention to the connected whole instead of just focusing on one piece.

Like when coyotes were continually breaking into their chicken coop and killing thirty to forty chickens in one night. John's instinct is to kill the coyote, remove the problem, which he does one day. But he doesn't feel right about what he's done. Plus, more and more coyotes soon follow.

But then by paying attention, observations turn into revelations. Like when John's gut feeling that coyotes are needed on the farm is confirmed when he realizes that their massive gopher problem, with the rodents eating the roots to their profitable fruit trees, is being curtailed by the coyotes. Then he realizes the coyotes that he saw as a problem were the answer to his gopher problem, and he actually wished he had more on the farm.

But still, what to do about protecting the chickens from being massacred by the coyotes? Some revelations are hard earned. Like horrifically finding out one night that one of his massive mastiff sheepdogs has killed their favorite old rooster, Greasy. But then noticing that their other mastiff doesn't touch the chickens and likes chasing the coyotes. So John puts that sheepherding mastiff in charge of protecting the chicken coop, which that mastiff does with mastery far beyond what John could've even accomplished sitting there all night with a shotgun.

Most of us fail, and then try to forget, avoid, or pretend that the failure never actually happened. John Chester began realizing that the failure was an integral part of the success as a whole. If he made a rash decision to remove the problem, he might be making a decision to destroy the health of the whole.

Starts with the Soil

There's a higher chance for life to thrive if the soil is healthy. So as we employ the Farmer Mindset Model, we must also pay attention to the soil.

This can be literal. We experience something magically grounding by digging in the earth. Go figure. Instead of jumping on social media to dig into the latest sensationalized "dirt" from the latest scandal, we'd be much better off going into the backyard and digging in our own actual dirt.

Putting your hands to the soil. Grabbing a shovel. Planting. Tending. Pruning. Raking. Watching tiny seeds become bountiful tomatoes. Feeding my soul, while feeding my body with fresh nutrients, which then in turn feeds my mind. It's all connected. Working the soil literally feeds your soul while you feed your mind and body. That's a full ecosystem win-win-win.

For me, while living in apartments, this started as a patio garden and pots on a ledge. It doesn't have to be big or elaborate to mean something. When we bought a house, this expanded into reseeding my lawn by hand, focusing on building the health of the soil back up before any grass seed was planted. And now I'm picking up yards of soil in my grandpa's '75 Ford pickup. The truck spent so many years at a farm, so it feels like I'm taking it back to its roots. I'm using the soil for a raised garden bed extension project I've been building in between writing this book to keep enriching my "Soul Soil" so it doesn't feel depleted as I write.

> It's those tiny revelations that are born from failure that act as a fuel for the engine of our ecosystem. And if I'm paying attention, I get to use it.
>
> —John Chester

> To forget how to dig the earth and to tend the soil is to forget ourselves.
>
> —Gandhi

As the growing season comes to an end now, this season we've grown eggplants, zucchinis, squash, pumpkins, carrots, chives, basil, peppers, and so oh so many delicious kinds of tomatoes. It nourished my soul to plant them and watch them grow, and nourishes our bodies to eat them.

We as a culture have become pretty consistent at constantly extracting from our soil without giving back to it, both figuratively and literally. We break the cycle and ecosystem of our earth's soil and our Soul's Soil by demanding much and giving back little. Extracting without replenishing.

We also feed the health of our Soul Soil by enriching it with life.

Wendell Berry is the prime example of this lifestyle and the Farmer Mindset Model. Berry is an activist, poet, writer, and "simple" Kentucky farmer whose life and message seem to resonate more clearly and precisely as each year passes.

"No use talking about getting enlightened or saving your soul," he wrote to his friend, the poet Gary Snyder, in 1980, "if you can't keep the topsoil from washing away."[3]

Which of course is a literal statement from Berry, as he has gone to war with his pen and voice against industrial farming, which he argues is stripping the earth of all its nutrients and destroying the land.

As Paul Kingsnorth described Berry in the foreword he wrote introducing Berry's essay collection *The World-Ending Fire: The Essential Wendell Berry*:

Wendell Berry's formula for a good life and a good community is simple and pleasingly unoriginal. Slow down. Pay attention. Do good work. Love your neighbors. Love your place. Stay in your place. Settle for less, enjoy it more.[4]

154

Yet, Wendell Berry's intentionally chosen "traditional" path is one that's becoming more and more radical. To slow down, pay attention, and stay. In a world of movers and shakers, staying anywhere for anything when the grass is greener somewhere else is as out of place as using a flip phone.

Hard Decisions and the Farmer Mindset Model

Why all this talk about hard decisions and farming?

Decisions are not made in an isolated vortex. When you make a hard decision with wisdom and the whole in view, or if you make a rash decision to escape something no matter the cost, the whole will also be affected. Your life is an ecosystem.

For example, let's say you've been making some hard decisions in life based on what's solely best for your career and nothing else. Then you begin to notice how many hours your boss works, how much money they've made, and how they're working through the aftermath of their second divorce and now splitting all the money they've made all kinds of ways—that's something to pay attention to.

> Decisions are not made in an isolated vortex . . . Your life is an ecosystem.

Maybe it's not about having a successful career in spite of other important aspects of your life. Maybe it's working toward building a thriving, healthy, successful life, and a career is one leg of the four-legged stool. When making career decisions, you need to make whole-life decisions. Your career fitting into your life instead of living your life being sick and tired from unsuccessfully keeping up with your career.

Or you start becoming laser-focused on "needing" to buy a bigger house in a "better" neighborhood so your kids can have a "better" life. You'll do whatever it takes. Then you start realizing that whatever it takes means overpaying by $150,000 and increasing your monthly mortgage by $2,000. Which means all financial margin you had in life will be removed, which really means all margin you had with your time will be gone. You're buying this house for "your kids." Sure, now your kid will have their own room. Great. But your kids won't be seeing their parents in their house because both parents will need to work much more to pay for the bigger house that's somehow supposed to bring the family closer together.

When I made a decision to quit baseball my senior year, I didn't know right then and there that the decision would directly lead to my first taste at what I wanted to do with my life, my first job, and then meeting the love of my life.

I made that decision not knowing or understanding the outcome. I made the decision toward health. I felt at that point in time that my life was out of whack. My ecosystem was sick. I needed to make a decision toward whole health instead of forcing this final year of baseball to happen because that's what I was "supposed to do."

It might be a hard decision toward wholeness and health, but honestly, should it be that hard of a decision if we're really paying attention to the health of the soil?

"What good will it be for someone to gain the whole world, yet forfeit their soul? Or what can anyone give in exchange for their soul?" (Matthew 16:26 NIV; see Mark 8:36). Jesus said these words, and both Matthew and Mark wrote them down. They really paid attention to them. Maybe we should as well. Like a farmer kneeling down and picking up a handful of dirt. Studying it for life. Seeking to understand what soil amendment is needed to strengthen the health of the soil. To benefit the whole.

To employ the Farmer Mindset Model, we pay attention to the "health of the whole" when making decisions. Making the right decisions in the right time.

The **FARMER MINDSET MODEL** means paying attention to the time and season that decisions need to be made, all with the "health of the whole" in mind.

156

Farmer Mindset Model

Hard Decision

What will you give up?

What will you gain?

What needs to die for something important to grow?

FOURTEEN

Writer Mindset Model

Reawakening one's awareness in the
pursuit of truth. Then, writing it all down!
Observations that lead to revelations.

Because this business of becoming conscious, of being a
writer, is ultimately about asking yourself, "How alive am
I willing to be?"

—Anne Lamott

I often tell people that everyone should write a book.

I also follow that up by saying writing a book will be the best,
and worst, thing to ever happen to you.

Because this stuff is hard. At least it is for me, and most ordi-
nary people, I think. I'm not one of those writers who is getting
excited about my adjective order and whether or not I should
split my infinitive.

I'm not pumping out pages like Schwarzenegger in the weight room doing curls for the girls.

I'm struggling to put words down. And I'm always messing around with *something*. Where I'm sitting; music or no music; the music is too loud, now it's too soft; I need more coffee; maybe if I ate an apple, that would help; checking my email now is probably a smart choice; man, I need to organize those shelves over there; how about a walk now; watch some funny comedians on YouTube for inspiration; all right, now I'm ready to really do this . . . oh wait, now it's lunch. I'll be back in an hour . . . okay, actually sometime tomorrow . . .

So why is writing so hard? Why do writers who are good at writing and get paid to write, still having to battle the urge to escape the act of writing? And why do us writers who struggle secretly despise any writers who act like the words just flow out of them like Niagara Falls.

For one, writing takes your full attention. It's really hard to be multitasking while writing. Actually it's impossible. Anything we have to give our full attention to is going to be a struggle.

Also it can be so hard to put words down and define how you think or feel in a straightforward way. It's painful—literally painful—at times. We all think we know what we feel or think until we have to write it down. Then it's, "Umm, yeah . . . so . . . these truths we hold . . . umm . . . oh so . . . no . . . look at that bird over there . . ."

We're all writers. Whether or not you'll ever write a book, we're all engaged in this craft in one way or another. Sure, most of our writing is done in text and email form or one hundred comments deep on some obscure Reddit thread about giant goldfish they're finding in the sewer. But how can thinking like a writer and practicing the Writer Mindset Model help us listen to our day and find insights for our life?

The Power of the Pond

Henry David Thoreau is one of the most renowned American authors with his book *Walden: Or, Life in the Woods*. Unsure of

> Rather than love, than money, than fame, give me truth.
>
> —Henry David Thoreau, *Walden*

his next steps after graduating Harvard and experiencing failure after an attempt to set up a school with his brother who became ill, Thoreau built a small cabin for himself on over sixty acres of land owned by his friend, and slightly well-known poet in his own right, Ralph Waldo Emerson. He lived there for over two years in an attempt to get away, seek a simpler life, search for his spirituality, and most importantly, look for truth. It was there he wrote *Walden*.

A writer must fight, scratch, claw, and crawl toward truth. Whether it be in life's absurdities and contradictions, in sorrow and mourning, or in joy and the fullness of life, the writer fights to shine light on truth. In this pursuit, the writer must stand at attention. The writer must be awake or, if sleeping, be attentive to their dreams.

> A writer must fight, scratch, claw, and crawl toward truth.

The writer is looking for the greater story. Always looking for the story within the story. Whether it is a novelist, a journalist, or someone who pens devotionals, the writer is searching for the deeper why, the message, the way of understanding that must be revealed to oneself before it can be revealed to others. It's a deeply personal and intense journey that takes their most raw and vulnerable thoughts and then shows them to the world.

A writer searches for truth. Sees the truth. Then aims to reveal the truth to whomever will take the time with them to pay attention. A writer invites others to *Come and take a look, right over there. Do you see it?*

A writer takes time to notice. Is always looking. And strives to never let busyness get in the way of revelation. We never know

160

We must learn to reawaken and keep ourselves awake, not by mechanical aids, but by an infinite expectation of the dawn, which does not forsake us even in our soundest sleep. I know of no more encouraging fact than the unquestionable ability of man to elevate his life by a conscious endeavor.

–Henry David Thoreau, *Walden*

when truth will pop up. It's typically when we least expect it. We must take time to see it and then write it down.

I find that some of my best writing happens when I'm not writing. It's when I'm living awake and aware to the truth swirling around me. I'm living in a masterpiece, and all I'm doing is taking notes so I can describe it to you.

Similar to a scientist or biologist, a writer studies what they see. Like Louis Agassiz who famously had a new student study a fish for hours and report all that he saw back to the professor. When the student, who quickly became impatient and tired of staring at one fish for hours, told the professor what he saw, Agassiz quite agitatedly responded to the student, "You have not looked very carefully; why?"

This went on the next day. Then the next. And the next. At one point the student started drawing the fish and Agassiz responded excitedly,

"That is right," said he, "a pencil is one of the best eyes."

The student had stared at and studied the fish for a week. But what started as an exercise in futility began to open the student's eyes as to all the things he'd missed seeing before. He was learning to see and pay attention to details and truths that escaped him before. He was seeing the beauty, the nuance, and the intricate creation that was this little fish.

161

Agassiz brought out another member of the fish family. Then another. All the while, the student faithfully studying and comparing the fishes, then reporting his findings to his professor. The student ended his account of the experience by saying,

> At the end of eight months, it was almost with reluctance that I left these friends and turned to insects; but what I gained by this outside experience has been of greater value than years of later investigation in my favorite groups.[1]

Taking Notes

When I'm writing a new book, I start by taking notes. I keep a list of notes all in one place that I add to throughout the day. Not organized. Not edited. Sometimes nonsensical, sometimes profound. But they are there. Many a writer will tell you there's no such thing as such a profound thought that you will actually remember it four hours later when you sit down and write!

All the ideas you thought you'd surely remember, you can't see when staring at the blank white screen. Like trying to spot your white dog in a blizzard. You know he's out there, but heck if you can see him.

The beauty of taking notes is, when I sit down to write a book, I'm not looking at a blank page. I'm looking at words, thoughts, and ideas. I've been placing kindling in the campfire all day, and now I just need to work on creating the spark. I've been doing the work all along by simply paying attention to what each day has told me.

Because writing doesn't happen when you're writing. Writing happens when you live in a way where you are simply seeing the words that are swirling around you every day and giving them space to grow.

The Writer and the Comedian

Actively paying attention and writing down thoughts and observations is where the craft of the comedian starts as well.

> Comedians are never really on vacation because you're always at
> attention . . . your antennae is always out there.
>
> —Bob Newhart

Comedians have this special gift, don't they? To make people laugh for an hour when they are paying money to come and laugh for an hour has to be one of the most difficult works of magic and art to pull off.

What's their secret? Are comedians coming up with far-reaching, radical ideas that no one has ever thought of during their routines? Not usually.

Their gift is recognizing and highlighting the great absurdity, ridiculousness, and hilariousness of everyday life. Comedians shine the light on something we have seen every day but have never really noticed. They see something ridiculous in their everyday lives and they write it down.

Comedians pay attention to the paradoxes and the peculiarities. They mine the magic of the mundane for hilarity by paying close attention to it and taking notes. Because maybe something's there for their next stand-up routine? Maybe not? Then, they invite others to laugh with them at what they've all seen together. There's a sense of community in a comedy act.

It all starts with paying attention and writing it down. Then comedians present their revelation onstage and listen for laughter to confirm if the audience has seen it too.

Superhuman Observation

When Thoreau died, many of his obituaries lauded him as "an original thinker" and "a man of simple tastes, hardy habits, and of preternatural powers of observation."

I don't think Thoreau's observation powers were superhuman. I think he took the time to pay attention longer than most. Like the

163

student staring at the fish. If you look at something long enough, you're going to see more things than anyone else.

In a culture that is obsessed with experts, it's not like all these people are gifted with a superhuman intellect. They've simply sat and studied one thing longer than others have. An expert is someone who has paid attention to one thing for a long time and is reporting back to us their findings.

There are aha moments all around you waiting to be seen. We just need to take note of them. That's what the **Writer Mindset Model** is—*to reawaken one's awareness in the pursuit of truth. Then, when you see it, write it all down!* It's living a life with observations leading to revelations.

Truth is not always what we want it to be. Truth might smack us square in the face and defy everything we thought was true. But if you look for truth, pay attention to it, and study it, you'll see the truth at some point. But we have to be willing to peel back the corner of the blanket and see what's hiding under there.

I want you to pay attention to the details of your day and what it is telling you. Insights. Ideas. Something that strikes you in a conversation or when reading an article. Then write it down. It doesn't have to be some philosophical, life-changing truth solving all the world's problems. (But if you spot those, by all means, write them down.) No, it can be a simple observation that strikes you as important in some way.

Then the real power of the Writer Mindset Model is in the follow-up "why." I'll call it the Writer's Why—where the observation turns into a revelation.

Examples like

I didn't get enough sleep last night and now my day is really suffering. What do I need to change to get better sleep and why do I keep repeating this pattern even though it dramatically affects me every day?

I always said that I didn't want to end up like my parents, yet as I'm with these two little kids all day, I act exactly like my parents did. Why is that? What was the good and the bad my parents taught me about parenting from their actions?

Wow, did I get extremely angry just then. It was something so small, yet I made it so big. I went from 1 to 15 at the drop of a fork. Why? What was that conversation touching on that really struck a way-too-reverberating chord with me? Where is this anger coming from?

Look at how happy that bird is. Just singing away, not worried one bit about the dangers lurking above or below. Just faced toward the sun and singing. I want to sit in the sun and sing more often. Why do I find it so hard to be at peace with my day? What am I so worried about? Is this worry real or is it something I've made to be a bigger worry than it is?

Taking notes and being an active participant in your life can be life changing. It's hard to be unintentional about what is really important to you when you're actually writing it down. Heck, who knows, maybe this is the beginning for your book. As you pay attention and take notes, maybe you'll see the book that's been waiting for you to write all along. Or you'll start spotting insights that will help you lead a richer, more meaningful life. Either works!

Write down ideas, thoughts, and truths that come at you today like a writer fighting to be aware of the observations that lead to revelation. Then, think about the Writer's Why—why is this important to you?

As you continue to take notes, I also want you to choose one day in your life to write about. Tell the story of an average day

Writing is the only way I have to explain my own life to myself.
—Pat Conroy

in your life. From the moment you get up to the moment you fall asleep. What emotions do you feel? What do you see and appreciate? What do you love about your day? What bothers or frustrates you? What guilty, nagging feeling can you not let go of that always makes you feel like you're failing your day, every day? I want you to go through the exercise of defining your day so you can see it in writing.

I'll repeat what Agassiz said: "That is right, a pencil is one of the best eyes."

Then take it a step further. I want you to write about what you'd like your day to be like twenty years from now, like you're living it in first person. *I get up at 7:00 a.m. and go down to the kitchen of my house to make coffee . . .* What are you doing? What are you seeing? What are you experiencing? Who are you doing it with? What are you paying attention to?

My mentor Ray Rood again had me do this exercise when I was struggling with lost hope and vision for my future. Writing about my life twenty years from now was this amazing exercise to pull my eyes away from the all-encompassing immediate and into what was possible. That's what good writing does. Not good in the sense of your adjectives all being in the correct order and your masterly use of perfect participles. No, good in the sense of transporting yourself to another place that is closer to reality and truth than where you currently sit.

> The **WRITER MINDSET MODEL** is awakening one's awareness in the pursuit of truth. Then, writing it all down! Observations that lead to revelations.

Writer Mindset Model

Thoughts, Ideas, Truths

"Writer's Why"

Thoughts, Ideas, Truths

"Writer's Why"

To reawaken one's awareness in the pursuit of truth.
Then, write it all down!

FIFTEEN

Consultant Mindset Model

Analyzing your day to understand what's working,
what's broken, and what needs to be changed.

> What would you say . . . you do here?
> —Bob, interviewing employee,
> *Office Space*

Bob and Bob. Two of the most famous fictional consultants from the acclaimed cult-classic *Office Space*. They are maybe not the best example of what a good consultant does, since their recommendations and helping "fix the glitch" of disgruntled employee Milton losing his paycheck (and his red stapler) ultimately led to the entire office building being burned down. But consultants in real life can play a very helpful role in assessing the health of an organization.

Yet, what do consultants *actually* do? Bob should be asking that question to himself.

Consultants are usually brought in as an outside perspective to see what's working, what's not working, and how things can be done better.

For those in the company, bringing in consultants can either be a really exciting, helpful endeavor or an extremely frightening and frustrating one. Because a good consultant should ultimately be striving to find the truth within the organization. They should be unbiased (not always the case because someone has hired them and brought them in). They should be on a fact-finding mission to be able to recognize all the various trees in the forest that the company operates in, determining which are healthy and which are sick.

When I worked as a marketing specialist for an organization, we brought in outside consultants to help us analyze what was and was not working. Let me tell you, I sat in some *very* awkward meetings during the week they were there. They were not afraid to ask the really tough questions. They were not afraid to press issues. They were relentless toward their pursuit of the truth. They had no loyalties and they weren't looking to play a game of politics. They were on a hunt for the truth based off the data and observations they were making.

Were they also tactful when doing it? Not necessarily. Most of the time those meetings felt like they were swinging more wrecking ball than olive branch. And when people feel like a wrecking ball is being swung in their vicinity, not surprisingly, they are going to do whatever it takes to escape.

When we made it to the end of the process with the consultants, they identified many broken systems and structures that needed to

My greatest strength as a consultant is to be ignorant and ask a few questions.

—Peter Drucker, management guru

be fixed or replaced. Their observations and recommendations led to many important changes that helped the organization's system run more effectively and efficiently.

Be Your Own Consultant

I want you to observe and analyze your day today like a consultant. How? Go on a fact-finding mission and pay attention to the data of your day. Be relentless and ruthless. Just look for the facts and cut out the fluff. *The* **Consultant Mindset Model** *is analyzing your day to understand what's working, what's broken, and what needs to be changed.*

Where are the inefficiencies of your day? Do you say you're going to get up at 7:00 a.m., but you actually got up at 8:00? The reason you got up an hour late was that you said you needed to go to sleep at 10:30 p.m. the night before, but you fell into bed at 12:30 after you sufficiently wasted two whole hours doing stuff that you can't even remember now.

> Time is a valuable commodity. If you've built the habit of simply wasting time to make it through the day, how are you going to progress to anything bigger and better?

How many hours of your workday are you actually working? If you really got after it, could you do all the work that you spread out for an entire day in a couple of hours? If so, what are you doing with all the time you're wasting? Is there anything more productive or purposeful you can be doing?

Learn a new skill. Ask your boss for a project in an area you enjoy. Time is a valuable commodity. If you've built the habit of simply wasting time to make it through the day, how are you going to progress to anything bigger and better? As a husband and dad now of four kids, I'll go ahead and throw out there that you'll never have as much time as you do right now. If you get married and have kids, each new addition slices your time pie chart up like the guy behind the counter slices up a pepperoni and sausage.

You have to honestly analyze your day. If you don't, who will? No one is going to force you to live the best life you can live.

Delight. Disdain. Do.

As you analyze your days like a consultant and try to figure out where you should be spending more of your time and less, three categories you can focus on are Delight, Disdain, Do.

What parts of your day do you delight in? Write them down. These are the parts of your day you look forward to and feel the most energized by. Typically as well, these are the parts of your day in which you're the most productive. If you don't feel like enough of your day fits in this space, can you shift or pivot any parts of it to live and breathe more in this space of delight? Enjoyment and love breed productivity and purpose. You can grit your teeth and continue to get things done that you actually hate doing. But really, how productive are you? How long can you keep up continually doing things that you can't stand doing? Sure, even in jobs you love, there will be parts you don't always enjoy. But the more you can shift your time spent doing those things you delight in, the more productive and peaceful your days will be. Call me an entitled millennial, but I've never quite understood the reasoning behind doing something you hate for fifty years, so that one day, when you retire, you can possibly do something you enjoy. Then when you get there, you actually have no idea what you actually enjoy, so you do things that retired people do that you actually don't enjoy that much. Oh, the joy.

Instead, put on your consultant hat, figure out the skills and strengths you delight and excel in, and construct your day to incorporate more of those.

What parts of your day do you disdain? These are the parts of your day you dread doing. Write them down. Again, I know that every day, all day is not going to be skipping through the park, eating Nutella-filled croissants and sipping cold brew. We all know there are those parts of your day you're going to have to grit your teeth and get through. It's part of work and life.

For me, it's emails. Gosh, I just don't like all the emails. Simply admitting the fact feels liberating to me. I don't like opening my inbox. I actively avoid it. For me, I relate it to when I used to read readers' reviews of my books on Amazon. I thought it would be a good exercise to read feedback that would then make me a better writer. Then I read enough of them (and thankfully they are mostly positive) to know that the best way to ruin your day is to read how much a stranger hates you, every word you put down, and what you wore while you wrote it.

It got to the point that every time I'd see a new review pop up, I'd shudder as I scrolled down to read it. It was like driving by a horrific car crash. You don't really want to see what happened, but you can't look away.

I feel the same way about my inbox at times. It's like, what fun gem is going to be waiting in there to grenade my day and make me question every decision I've made about life? Maybe I'm being a little overdramatic about it, but I'd definitely throw it in the disdain category.

My wife, Naomi, on the other hand, loves email. She probably checks her inbox a hundred times a day. It's in her Delight sweet spot. So you know what, she checks mine too and tells me when something's come in that I need to respond to. It works well for us.

Obviously you might not have a spouse who will check your email for you, but are there ways for you to reduce the hours doing what you disdain? Can you outsource or ask for help doing tasks you can't stand? Can you start working with your manager or boss to accomplish more tasks in your Delight box than your Disdain one?

Double up on the delight of your day by doing less of what you disdain. Sure, if it's week two of a new job, you might not have much leverage to start having those conversations. But if you continually show productivity and excellence doing those things you love, you're going to get a chance to do more of it.

Now comes the Do category. What parts of your day are you just doing stuff that you don't necessarily disdain or delight in? What parts of your day are you just going through the motions? Write them down.

Is there any way for you to shift something you just do into something you delight in? Driving to work could be in the Do category. But what if you left thirty minutes early and rode your bike instead? Would that become something you look forward to and delight in?

Eating lunch is something that could be in your Do category. How can you switch it to Delight? Maybe instead of rushing to grab whatever you can find, you spend more time preparing and planning for your lunches, making yourself something healthy. Maybe during lunch you become more intentional about taking out someone you want to connect with and spend more time with.

We don't have to go through our days just doing stuff. We can be more strategic and align what we need to do with what we delight in.

So like a good consultant, I want you to employ the **Consultant Mindset Model** and take an audit of your day. Obviously, being your own consultant is not exactly how it's supposed to work, but I want you to go on a fact-finding mission about your day like you are an outside consultant and analyze your day. Focus on four categories: *Delight. Disdain. Do. And Do More Of.*

The **CONSULTANT MINDSET MODEL** is analyzing your day to understand what's working, what's broken, and what needs to be changed.

Consultant Mindset Model

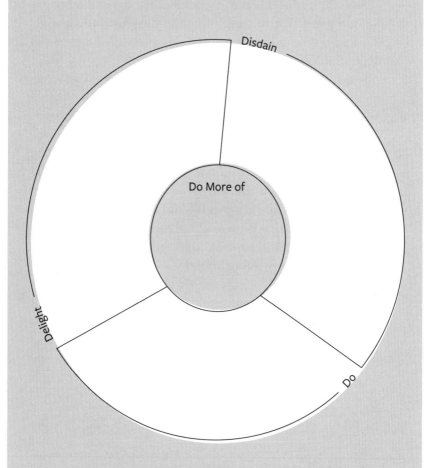

SIXTEEN

Investigator Mindset Model

Observing and analyzing data and
patterns within your day to form
hypotheses and conclusions as you better
understand the true story of your life.

The world is full of obvious things which nobody by any
chance ever observes.

—Sir Arthur Conan Doyle

Investigators are on an all-encompassing, uncompromising search
for the truth. They take in a massive amount of data, observations,
and clues to deduce "what really is taking place here."

How are investigators getting to the truth through their observations? Similar to the Consultant in a way, an Investigator
is taking the process a step further as they are observing and
analyzing the data in search for the pattern. Consistency and
truth are found in the pattern. It's not random. It's not sprouting

out of nowhere. Investigators are paying attention to the context of the whole to understand the pattern embedded within that leads to truth.

Naomi is constantly viewing her day through patterns. She's always on the lookout for them. When she's observing strangers, she's usually analyzing them by the patterns she's noticing as she seeks to understand their backstory. If it appears like Naomi is "zoned out," she's probably creating someone's backstory in her head based off patterns she's observed.

She's got some Sherlock in her DNA, apparently. Things are typically more connected than we see initially. By understanding the pathway of patterns, we can better understand the truth.

Sherlock's Superpower

If you've watched one episode of the many Sherlock spinoffs or happened to read one of Sir Arthur Conan Doyle's original Sherlock books, you've experienced Sherlock's incredible skill for deducing the truth based off his observations. Sherlock has been relevant and timely for nearly 150 years, with him even receiving a Guinness World Record for "having been depicted on screen 254 times . . . [being] awarded a world record for the most portrayed literary human character in film & TV."[1]

Why have so many generations across continents loved Sherlock so much? I think it's because we're awed by him and want to be like him. To have that incredible gift of observation that can tell you the plain truth of a situation like you're reading an open book.

Sherlock possessed the superpower of paying attention. What was the essence of his powers? They are immense, but they are also very straightforward and simple. The skill of Sherlock is observing the small to deduce something big and meaningful from the pattern. As Sherlock lamented of others not willing to employ this same mindset, "You see but you do not observe."[2]

So how do we employ and practice the Investigator Mindset Model in our lives? Do we go out into our neighborhoods and start solving the latest crimes posted on NextDoor of the mysterious man discovered drinking a latte in someone's garage at 1:00 a.m.? We could.

Instead, what if we turned this investigative lens and looked at our feelings through it?

Let's investigate the facts of your feelings.

Patterns to Your Feelings

Feelings aren't fleeting. They are not pulled out of thin air or fabricated. Feelings are based on facts. They're based on a foundation of thoughts, beliefs, and ideas. Your feelings are a by-product of a thought your mind has taken hold of. Feelings do not exist outside of thought. We have separated the heart and the head, but is that actually the case?

Sometimes our feelings can be mysterious. Like going to the doctor and trying to pinpoint where the pain is. "Can you tell me exactly where it hurts." You know you're in pain. It's somewhere over here. But, gosh, now that you're being asked to precisely locate it, the pain point seems ambiguous.

Our feelings can be the same way. Then we're acting on feelings that we don't quite understand.

> Feelings aren't fleeting. They are not pulled out of thin air or fabricated. Feelings are based on facts. They're based on a foundation of thoughts, beliefs, and ideas.

As the late Dallas Willard wrote, "It is extremely difficult for most people to recognize which ideas are governing their life and how those ideas are governing their life. . . . To understand anything, of course, some intelligent attention and methodical inquiry is required."[3]

Dallas Willard, the philosopher, theologian, professor, and author, is sounding a lot like Sherlock here. "Intelligent attention" and "methodical inquiry." Sherlock would've been proud.

What if we employed these investigative skills to pay attention to our feelings? Really, to understand our feelings we have to understand our thoughts. Like Sherlock, we must observe the pattern and clues. Sherlock always knew that the deceased body did not just magically appear in the field. Something brought it there. All he needed to do was observe the clues to lead him back to the source.

Crack the Case to Your Feelings

When we fail to understand our feelings, we're sometimes failing to observe and understand the pattern of thoughts and by-product actions that are leading us to that feeling.

Seeking to understand is the pathway to wisdom. It's understanding where the well is and how you fill it with something good. *The* **Investigator** **Mindset Model** *is observing and analyzing data and patterns within your day to form hypotheses and conclusions as you better understand the true story of your life.*

This is what you pay good money to do in counseling, right? You are feeling a certain way. Typically, a negative emotion. You don't usually see people running to counseling because they are feeling overwhelming amounts of joy that they want to comprehend better.

No, there is some overwhelming negative emotion that is sitting on your chest like your seventh-grade bully who won't let you up. But you don't understand where this bully is coming from and why they are sitting on your chest.

You don't understand *why* you are feeling *that* way. And the weight of the unknown is crushing you.

I remember a moment after college when I was living in Santa Barbara, working a good job, making a living, yet sitting in my car overlooking the beautiful Pacific Ocean and just bawling. Not happy tears, but mournful tears coming from a place I didn't understand. Then I felt quite guilty for feeling sad. Here I was in paradise, crying? What did I have to feel sad about? I couldn't understand what was going on inside me. I was missing the pattern. I was failing to recognize what thoughts and beliefs were leading me to this place. Something was severely missing, and I was severely missing what exactly it was. It was a helpless feeling.

So I sought counseling for the first time. The psychologist or counselor is helping you *investigate* the facts to your feelings. They are helping you uncover the belief system and thought process that are leading to these feelings. A counselor is guiding you to pay attention to the "pathway pattern" leading you to this place.

We don't instantly just change the way we feel. We change the way we think and what we believe, which changes the way we feel. We have to bring a level of awareness and understanding to our feelings, so that we better see why we're feeling the way we feel.

Two people could go through the exact same experience and feel two completely different ways about it. Two students who are friends could be sitting side by side next to each other as a teacher implores them to do better work and study harder. One student may feel challenged by this reprimand because they believe that the teacher is in fact right. They haven't been putting in the work, and they believe they are capable of doing big things. Their parents have always challenged them in love, always affirming in them the skills and strengths they see in them, but not letting them slide by with laziness or pride. They know they are capable of doing great work. This belief system will take the criticism as a challenge.

The other student feels the exact opposite from the teacher's reprimand. This student feels hurt and offended. *How dare this teacher question my work ethic.* The only time their parents talk about their schoolwork is when they happen to bring home a bad grade. Then they are yelled at and belittled for being stupid and lazy. This student feels crushed by the criticism, because if they are being honest with themselves, they believe they aren't capable of much.

Both students experiencing the same thing, with complete opposite feelings as the product, based off opposite beliefs as the foundation. One student leaves feeling challenged and emboldened to work harder. The other student feels crushed and ashamed. It was the same reprimand that was experienced in two different ways through two different lenses.

Investigate the Pattern Pathway to Your Feelings

Let's put on our Sherlock hat today. If you want to don a cape and pipe as well to get you in the mind space, feel free.

Let's do some investigative work right now as we employ the Investigator Mindset Model. Let's investigate the facts to your feelings to understand the pathway of patterns. Again, feelings are a by-product of thoughts and beliefs. Listen and observe your day like an investigator to see the pattern and better understand the source of your feelings.

Joy. Frustration. Peace. Anger. Sadness. Disgust. Exhilaration. Pain. Helplessness. Guilt. Shame. Boredom. Excitement. Contentment. Gratitude. There are a lot of feelings to be all up in throughout the day. Let's see and observe. Let's make note of the feelings we are experiencing today and then do some investigative work on the pattern of why we might be feeling this way—both negatively and positively.

I want you to pay attention to your feelings today. Especially if there are certain feelings you've been having lately that you haven't been able to define. If you can't find the source of a river, sometimes you have to investigate upstream.

Pay attention to the source today. Then investigate and look for the pattern. Look for the actions based off thoughts and beliefs taking place that are then leading you to feel a certain way.

For example, pay attention to your frustration and discontent. Frustration can be a great clarifier. What are you frustrated about today, and most importantly, why are you frustrated? What's the pattern there? What thought patterns need to be changed, and what are some different actions you can take accordingly?

Also, pay attention to your energy and joy. Example: I'm seeing a pattern that every time I'm working on a team, I feel joy. I really like collaborating with people, and I do it so rarely in my job. How do I incorporate more team dynamics in my job? Are there assignments I can volunteer to spearhead and then form a team around them? Is teamwork compatible with the career path I'm on? If not, I need to investigate roles and work that might be more suited toward this value of teamwork.

If we pay attention to and understand the pattern to our feelings, we can better understand the truth. Fill in the graphic below as you investigate throughout the day the "facts to your feelings." Are you discerning any trends or patterns to your thoughts and the feelings that follow?

The **INVESTIGATOR MINDSET MODEL** is observing and analyzing data and patterns within your day to form hypotheses and conclusions as you better understand the true story of your life.

Investigator Mindset Model

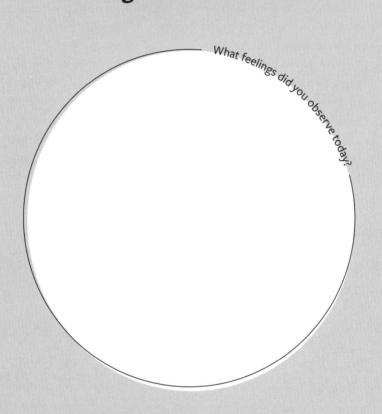

What feelings did you observe today?

What thoughts and beliefs preceded these feelings?

SEVENTEEN

Monk Mindset Model

Not constantly doing, but paying
attention to our being through reflection,
silence, prayer, and meditation.

> Silence is becoming an endangered species.
> —Nun, *The Mountain Life*
> (documentary)

Silence is an endangered species. We must fight to keep it alive. We must fight to protect it like we do the honeybees. Because without either, life will not go on.

Yet, the world does not want you to have silence. Commerce cannot thrive if you're not listening to it. Social platforms cannot grow if you're not paying attention to them.

If we are going to properly listen to our day, we must lend our ear to the soft and silent. To the whisper. The nudge. It's like our soul is raising its hand like a shy schoolchild and asking to be called upon. It has so much to say, but first we must see the hand and hear the voice.

Choosing silence is choosing to pay attention to your soul. It is nourishment and substance. Silence to your soul is like light and water is to a flower. We tend to the garden. How can we not tend to our soul?

We must construct some *silent silos* in our day. We must work to make silence a habit. Just like we would protect our vegetable garden from rodents so that they will not consume all our life-giving bounty, so we must protect our soul from all the noise that is trying to devour it.

> Choosing silence is choosing to pay attention to your soul.

This is what a monk does. Some monks might even take a vow of silence. Instead of continually hearing their own audible voice, they might hear the voice of their soul, which is being tended to by the Spirit. Monks are daily making communion with the natural and spiritual world around them. Through prayer and meditation, they are asking God to help them hear and see all that is nourishing to the soul. Monks are seeking the deep wellsprings of wisdom through silence, not through the banging cacophony of noise and disruption.

We are seemingly living through one upheaval after another, then we wonder why so many of us can't find our footing.

To be still and know. To seek silence so that we can hear. To live in peace, even if the ground around us is shifting and shaking. This is drawing from the deep well of wisdom.

To seek silence is to seek wisdom. To constantly seek noise and distraction is to run full speed down the path of fools, not noticing how many are dropping off the cliff in front of us.

We cannot make the best of what we are if our hearts are always divided between what we are and what we are not.
—Thomas Merton, Trappist monk

Foolishness diverts the course of life.

Proverbs 19:3

Whoever gains a wise heart loves his own soul,
  and whoever preserves understanding experiences true goodness.

Proverbs 19:8

Wisdom is not braggadocious. Wisdom is not haughty. Wisdom is not loud and in your face. To enter into the world of noise peacefully, we must come from a place of silence and rest.

Like I wrote in *25 Lies Twenty-somethings Need to Stop Believing*, "Silence speaks to your well-being, not your well-doing."[1] Silence is free and it brings freedom.

> To seek silence is to seek wisdom. To constantly seek noise and distraction is to run full speed down the path of fools.

Seeking Silence Outside

I've heard of many outdoor enthusiasts speaking of their times in nature as going to church. As I sit here in the same beat-up camping chair by the same lake I've written many a book, I reflect on the seminal memories in my life where my soul has felt nourished.

Fly-fishing in a stream by myself surrounded by the Rocky Mountains in Colorado. Watching the ripples on the water. Seeing the beautiful pinks on the side of a rainbow trout. Hearing the birds sing their songs of delight. Watching the cottonwood trees sway in the wind as thousands of white puffs fall into the water below like a midsummer snow.

I see the time in high school when Mike, Adam, and I walked to the top of a mountain ridge to watch the sun peek over the mountain across the valley as we stood together and prayed.

I see myself sitting next to my grandfather on a bucket at my uncle Russell's farm in Kansas as we threw our fishing line into the water and watched the cows slowly mosey up to the water to lean over and take a drink.

I see those times working at Deer Valley Ranch surrounded by a collection of 14,000-foot mountains called the Collegiate Peaks. Fitting, because so much of my education about the depth and breadth of life came from my summers working there. My boss Harold was president of the Colorado Mule Riders Association, and one time I was able to go with him as we packed supplies for Colorado forest workers to work on trails. We ventured deep in the mountains in the same manner they did in the 1800s when they first explored to try and catch a glimpse of the enormity of life and resources embedded in the inhabitable. Even with all the technology in the world at our fingertips, horses and mules quietly and surely finding their way in between massive pines and rocks is still the most effective way to venture into the depths of creation.

Beyond these big seminal memories where I purposefully removed myself from the world of noise into the quiet, I still see the silent moments in my day as the most nourishing. Of working in the garden and digging in the dirt. Going on a walk around the lake. Lying in the bathtub in stillness. Taking a hike. Spending those few quiet moments in the morning reading my Bible as I watch the water sprinklers shoot life to the green grass below. It's these moments where my well-being is fed. It's in the quiet where I hear the most truth, wisdom, and God's promptings in my life.

It's hard to hear someone talking to you if your ears are filled with noise from elsewhere. Same with our conversations with God. If our ears are constantly filled with noise from everywhere, and anywhere else, how can we hear his voice?

The Loudest Man Who Fought for the Most Silence

Teddy Roosevelt was probably one of the loudest, most frenetic, most energetic presidents the USA has ever known. He was constantly on the move. He fought head-on the vicious crime in New York, the slums, and torrid working conditions the working class were living and dying in. He took on the most powerful heads of the most powerful industries to fight against monopolies and the exploitation of commerce.

Teddy Roosevelt was the most public, vocal, and well-known man of his time and is probably the last person to ever be confused for a monk. Yet, he implemented federal protection for more natural landscapes and beauty than any president before or after. Teddy Roosevelt established preserves of over 230 million acres, including "150 national forests, 51 bird preserves, four national game preserves, five national parks and 18 national monuments." Think Yellowstone National Park, the Grand Canyon, and Yosemite National Park.[2]

Heck, children to this day still curl up in bed with Roosevelt's namesake as they turn off the lights and hold tight their stuffed bear. As the story goes, Roosevelt refused to shoot a bear that was tied up to a tree. The incident was turned into a political cartoon which led to the creation of a child's toy called "Teddy's Bear."

A man who was born in New York City fought to preserve nature and beauty for future generations to experience. He was also the man who was the youngest to be elected to the New York State Assembly at twenty-three years old,[3] but left his rapidly growing political career to find silence. A tragic night changed his life forever when his mother passed away from typhoid fever, and then, just hours later, his wife died from kidney failure. In his

There is delight in the hardy life of the open. There are no words that can tell the hidden spirit of the wilderness, that can reveal its mystery, its melancholy, and its charm.

—Teddy Roosevelt

journal, Roosevelt drew a large *X* and wrote, "The light has gone out of my life."[4]

Soon after, Roosevelt would purchase a claim in a ranch in the Dakotas and for the next few years would find himself living and working there as a cattle rancher. As he fought to heal, he immersed himself in nature and silence. He never forgot the transformative role both played in his life.

Feeding Our Body and Soul

We become ever more concerned, and we spend good money, on what we feed our body. How are we not even equally concerned about what we feed our soul?

Employing the **Monk Mindset Model** means *not constantly doing, but paying attention to our being through reflection, silence, prayer, and meditation.*

As we pay attention to the Monk Mindset Model, we must seek silent silos throughout our day. We won't be able to hear much if we never give ourselves the time and space to listen.

PRACTICE

Over the next few days, pay attention to start building the habit of creating silent silos in your day. Getting up from your computer and taking a walk. Not turning on talk radio in the car. Going on a hike and not listening to music. Getting up in the morning to journal and pray.

Write down what you hear in these spaces. Write down what you feel these moments of silence are doing for the substance of your soul. Seeking silence might be uncomfortable at first. Don't run from it. Force yourself to sit in it as long as you can. Starting with just five minutes a day.

Reflect and write down seminal memories in your life when you felt your soul most nourished. What were you doing? Or better put, what were you not doing? Do you remember what you felt in that time or what you heard? Write it down here.

The **MONK MINDSET MODEL** is not constantly doing, but paying attention to our being through reflection, silence, prayer, and meditation.

Monk Mindset Model

Not constantly doing, but paying attention to our being
through reflection, silence, prayer, and meditation.

Quiet Space

Quiet Space

Quiet Space

What did you hear?

What did you hear?

What did you hear?

Conclusion

A Life Lived Listening to Each Day

Don't seek to change your life. Seek to change your day, each day, which will change your life.

The best thing about the future is that it comes one day at a time.

—Abraham Lincoln

We have been given so many gifts for clarity each day. Now we know we have no excuse not to see or hear them. We can live this wild life, eyes and ears open to the truth, revelations, ideas, and wisdom found even in the most mundane of days. Our thoughts, experiences, and feelings all building off each other, culminating, weaving together this beautiful blend of our lives found in each day.

We don't have to feel stuck or powerless to change. We don't have to feel blind or confused. We can see each day for the revelation it is.

Being an active, engaged participant in your own life is the most important habit and gift you can give yourself. If you don't pay attention to your day, who will?

Abraham Lincoln and His Ability to Pay Close Attention

I look at someone like Abraham Lincoln. I know Lincoln is probably used as an example in more self-help books than most anyone, but hear me out. Studying Abraham Lincoln, reading the incredible book *Team of Rivals*, is like experiencing a master class on a person who paid incredible attention to the people in the room, the people in an entire nation, and the feelings swirling around inside him as he tried to lead a nation through its most difficult stretch of history. Lincoln is the prime example of someone who paid attention with an unbelievable ability to see his world through these various mindset models we've discussed in this book. As Pulitzer Prize–winning Doris Kearns Goodman describes:

> Lincoln possessed an uncanny understanding of his shifting moods, a profound self-awareness that enabled him to find constructive ways to alleviate sadness and stress. Indeed, when he is compared with his colleagues, it is clear that he possessed the most even-tempered disposition of them all.[1]

Really, Lincoln's greatest gift and skill, what made him the needed leader at such a crucial time, was his ability to pay close attention. He possessed and practiced an acute awareness of people, places, and his feelings and foibles, oftentimes telling a folksy story or self-deprecating joke that would land perfectly with his audience because he was aware of what his audience was looking for.

Lincoln understood that we see what we're looking for.

Studying Lincoln is watching someone operate from the various mindset models I've written about in this book. Lincoln can be seen bouncing back and forth between paying attention to the day as a Writer, Farmer, Investigator, Monk, and even as an Entrepreneur before politics.

Lincoln looked at the day through the Farmer Mindset as he understood timing, seasons, when it was time to plant and time to uproot. He could often be found telling a homespun farming story that everyone could relate to like talking about the power of a fly to motivate a horse.

Lincoln was an amazing writer and orator who used language in a way that people understood and were moved by. There were no speechwriters nor teleprompters. Just Lincoln on a train or in his study, writing down words that would reverberate through history.

While his friend and grand orator William Seward would be found speaking for hours, using the high and lofty language of a great intellectual, Lincoln would speak from a humble and understated place, reaching the heart of the average person through language and stories they could relate to.

One of Lincoln's most famous speeches, the Gettysburg Address, was delivered after the horrific yet tide-turning battle in Pennsylvania. And he delivered that powerful speech in three minutes. Do you know who spoke before Abraham Lincoln? I've read who did before and I still had to look it up. It was Edward Everett, who apparently was a very famous orator of his day. Lincoln spoke for three minutes, and his words were immortalized forever. I can still recite those first immortalized lines (even without the help of Google).

"Four score and seven years ago, our fathers brought forth a new nation conceived in liberty and dedicated to the proposition that all men are created equal . . ."

Those people who look for the bad in people will surely find it.
—Abraham Lincoln

Edward Everett spoke for two hours. Does anyone remember what he said? The only thing I've read about what he said was when speaking to Lincoln about his speech: "I wish that I could flatter myself that I had come as near to the central idea of the occasion, in two hours, as you did in two minutes."[2]

Lincoln often saw the world through the lens of a comedian just to survive and find humor amidst the daily atrocities he was constantly faced with. Oftentimes his analysis of serious occasions and matters was wrapped in humor. When addressing the lack of forward movement his general McClellan possessed, Lincoln stated, "I wish McClellan would go at the enemy with something—I don't care what. General McClellan is a pleasant and scholarly gentleman. He is an admirable engineer, but he seems to have a special talent for a stationary engine."[3]

An amazing orator and visible leader, Lincoln could be found retreating to his study for solace and solitude in the many trying times of his life and presidency. "I am rather inclined to silence, and whether that be wise or not, it is at least more unusual nowadays to find a man who can hold his tongue than to find one who cannot."[4]

Lincoln once shared a story of a lost farmer caught at night in a pitch-black thunderstorm. The farmer looked up to the sky and called out to God for help. The last line of his prayer was as pertinent to Lincoln as it is to us now: "Give us a little more light and a little less noise."[5]

We All Can Pay Attention

While there was only one Abraham Lincoln, there's also only one of you. Only one person who can pay attention to your life like you can. It's a gift and a responsibility.

No matter your station in life, your upbringing, the opportunities you've been given, the opportunities that have been stripped away, or the time and place in which this book finds you, you have the same power to pay attention. You have the same gift and opportunity to be actively engaged in your life. This is not for the chosen few. This is an open invitation to all of us to come in and join the party.

To pay attention. To see and hear.

Answers are swirling all around you. Like you're standing in a field of dandelions. As the winds swirl, you can run for cover or you can reach out and catch the dandelions floating all around you. To live life, hands, eyes, and hearts wide open. To see and understand the amazing gift of your life for what it is, and the amazing gift you can therefore offer others.

There's great gain in paying attention. We no longer have to be intentionally blind to the things that matter. To pay attention is to pay it forward with love, empathy, grace, and wisdom.

What payment will you make with your life? Will you pay your attention to worthy things that matter or worthless things that are purely designed to distract?

Will you pay attention to the "health of the whole" when making hard decisions?

Will you pay attention to the insights, ideas, and revelations that you are receiving throughout the day and write them down?

> There's great gain in paying attention. We no longer have to be intentionally blind to the things that matter.

Will you show love by paying attention to the people you say you love most?

Will you pay attention to the "pathway of patterns" that is creating the same feelings and emotions every day? Will you seek to understand why you are feeling that way by changing your thoughts that are leading to negative emotions?

Will you pay attention to your values and how they are being fed or starved throughout the day?

Will you pay attention to the problems you see throughout the day, and see them not as problems but as opportunities for action and creativity?

195

Will you pay attention to and protect those silent silos throughout the day where you have the opportunity to think, reflect, and pray?

Will you pay attention to the ways you are or are not feeding your soul as well as your body?

Will you pay attention to not making life more serious than it needs to be and choose to see the hilarity in the everyday?

Will you pay attention to the aspects of your day that you delight in and lean into those spaces more?

Will you choose to move from being intentionally blind to intentionally aware?

Will you begin the lifelong practice of paying attention?

Listening to Your Day, Every Day

This is my challenge to you and to me.

Your life is dripping with meaning. Put out your hands and catch all that is good. Pay attention and you will see. Listen and you will hear.

> Your life is dripping with meaning. Put out your hands and catch all that is good. Pay attention and you will see. Listen and you will hear.

The sights and sounds that await you are amazing. We can look for and really see the moonwalking bears now.

Write what listening to your day now looks like to you. What does listening to your day look like moving forward? Write that down and tape it to your bathroom mirror. What will you choose to pay attention to moving forward and what will you choose to not focus on? The choice and the challenge is now yours.

WHERE WILL YOU PAY ATTENTION?

Write below what you now want to focus your attention on every day and what you will choose not to focus on. Pay attention on purpose to what matters and watch your life feel much more purposeful.

Give us eyes to see. Give us ears to hear. So that we might understand.

I choose to pay attention to:

I choose to not pay attention to:

Big Thank-Yous

First, a huge thank-you to you! This book would've been extremely lonely without you. Thank you for taking the time to read this book. I hope it has been helpful for you. I'd be extremely honored if you shared about this book with friends on social media and left a review. These things make such a huge difference for the impact of this book and for myself. Thank you!

Connect with me and tag me on Twitter and Instagram @PaulAngone. I love connecting with you! Also you can find free chapters from all five of my books and lots more inspiring content at AllGroanUp.com, if you're looking for more good stuff.

Thank you to my wife Naomi who spent a lot of hours watching a lot of kids while I was away in Writing World. Thank you as well, Naomi, for reading through the book and editing it like you have for every book. Thank you for your love and support. None of my books happen without you.

Thank you again to my agent Chad Allen for the support and help making all this happen. From helping me flush out ideas to the nuts and bolts of it all. Thank you for always being a source of encouragement and wisdom.

Thank you to the wonderful team at Baker Publishing. From design, to sales, to marketing, to PR and editorial. Thank you specifically to my amazing editors Patnacia Goodman and Barbara Barnes. Thank you for your expertise and encouragement all the way through, for your editorial work and skill in making this book crisp, clean, and more readable!

Thank you again to John Irwin and the incredible people at the Downing House. For letting me stay again and write. For stewarding an incredibly peaceful and life-giving place. So much of this book happened here. Thank you.

As I do in every book, thank you to the musicians who encouraged me and became a soundtrack for me while I wrote this book. In books past, it's definitely been more of an eclectic mix of artists and songs that made an impact on me while I wrote. For this book, I found myself listening to a long line of Odesza and Porter Robinson's album "Nurture." While editing the book, Arcade Fire's song "Unconditional" was a source of encouragement and inspiration to me. Love that song. Thank you to these musicians for breathing so much life and energy into your songs, which in turn encouraged me to push through and create.

Notes

Introduction

1. Christopher Chabris, in Siri Carpenter, "Sights Unseen," American Psychological Association, April 2001, https://www.apa.org/monitor/apr01/blindness (emphasis mine).

2. "Test Your Awareness: Do the Test," Transport for London, https://www.youtube.com/watch?v=Ahg6qcgoay4.

3. Carpenter, "Sights Unseen."

Chapter One The Epic Journey Right Where You Are

1. Paolo Coelho, *The Alchemist* (New York: HarperOne, 1993), vii.

2. Paul Angone, *101 Secrets for Your Twenties* (Chicago: Moody, 2013), Secret 22.

3. *Cambridge Dictionary*, s.v. "awareness (*n.*)," https://dictionary.cambridge.org/us/dictionary/english/awareness.

Part One The Life-Changing Power of Paying Attention

1. Vance Packard, *The Hidden Persuaders* (Philadelphia: McKay, 1957), https://www.hoopladigital.com/play/11862081.

2. Dave Chappelle, interview on *CBS This Morning* with Gayle King, March 20, 2017.

Chapter Two The Lure of the Distraction

1. Paul Angone, *25 Lies Twentysomethings Need to Stop Believing* (Grand Rapids: Baker, 2021), 85.

2. Angone, *25 Lies*, 85.

3. Paul Angone, *101 Secrets for Your Twenties* (Chicago: Moody Publishers, 2013), 76.

Chapter Three Un-Dividing Our Divided Attention

1. "The Sirens," Greek Gods and Goddesses, February 7, 2017, https://greek godsandgoddesses.net/myths/the-sirens/.

2. Aza Raskin, quoted in Hilary Andersson, "Social Media Apps Are 'Deliberately' Addictive to Users," BBC, July 4, 2018, https://www.bbc.com/news/technology-44640959.

3. Raskin, quoted in Andersson, "Social Media Apps."

4. Cristiano Lima and Cat Zakrzewski, "Former Facebook Employee Frances Haugen Revealed as 'Whistleblower' behind Leaked Documents That Plunged the Company into Scandal," *Washington Post*, October 4, 2021, https://www.washingtonpost.com/technology/2021/10/03/facebook-whistleblower-frances-haugen-revealed/.

5. "Facebook Whistleblower Frances Haugen Testifies on Children and Social Media Use: Full Senate Hearing Transcript," Rev.com, https://www.rev.com/blog/transcripts/facebook-whistleblower-frances-haugen-testifies-on-children-social-media-use-full-senate-hearing-transcript.

6. Jena Hilliard, "What Is Social Media Addiction?," The Addiction Center, July 15, 2019, edited August 26, 2022, https://www.addictioncenter.com/drugs/social-media-addiction/.

7. Maria Konnikova, *The Confidence Game* (New York: Penguin, 2016), 10.

8. Elle Hunt, "Why It's Good to Be Bored," *The Guardian*, 2020, https://www.theguardian.com/global/2020/may/03/why-its-good-to-be-bored.

9. Minda Zetlin, "Taking Selfies Destroys Your Confidence and Raises Anxiety, a Study Shows. Why Are You Still Doing It?," *Inc.*, https://www.inc.com/minda-zetlin/taking-selfies-anxiety-confidence-loss-feeling-unattractive.html.

10. Jennifer Mills et al., "'Selfie' Harm: Effects on Mood and Body Image in Young Women," *Body Image* 27 (2018): 86–92.

11. Julia Naftulin, "Here's How Many Times We Touch Our Phones Every Day," Business Insider, 2016, https://www.businessinsider.com/dscout-research-people-touch-cell-phones-2617-times-a-day-2016-7.

12. Raskin, quoted in Andersson, "Social Media Apps."

13. James Clear, *Atomic Habits* (New York: Avery, 2018), 22.

Chapter Four Paying Attention to How You Pay Attention

1. Dallas Willard, *Renovation of the Heart* (Colorado Springs: NavPress, 2002), 95.

Chapter Five The Importance of Awkward, Boring, and Quiet Spaces

1. Bryan Robinson, "Why Neuroscientists Say, 'Boredom Is Good for Your Brain's Health," *Forbes*, 2020, https://www.forbes.com/sites/bryanrobinson/2020/09/02/why-neuroscientists-say-boredom-is-good-for-your-brains-health/?sh=10e2acb51842.

2. Paul Angone. *101 Questions You Need to Ask in Your Twenties* (Chicago: Moody, 2013), 97.

3. Doug Gelbert, "The Man in the Bathtub in Downtown Grand Junction," Uncover Colorado, 2020, https://www.uncovercolorado.com/dalton-trumbo-colorado-screenwriter/.

Chapter Six Paying Attention by Letting Your Mind Wander

1. Joshua Shepherd, "Why Does the Mind Wander?," *Neuroscience of Consciousness* 2019, no. 1 (2019), https://doi.org/10.1093/nc/niz014.

2. K. L. Merlo et al., "Qualitative Study of Daydreaming Episodes at Work," *Journal of Business and Psychology* 35 no. 2 (2020): 203–22.

3. Peter Gray, "The Value of Mind Wandering in Solving Difficult Problems," *Psychology Today*, February 7, 2019, https://www.psychologytoday.com/us/blog/freedom-learn/201902/the-value-mind-wandering-in-solving-difficult-problems.

Chapter Seven The Importance of Seminal Memories

1. Wendell Berry. "The Objective," *Look & See*, Two Bird Film, 2017.

2. Oliver Sacks, "Alzheimer's and the Power of Music," Alzheimer's & Dementia Weekly, http://www.alzheimersweekly.com/2013/06/alzheimers-power-of-music.html.

3. Sacks, "Alzheimer's."

Chapter Eight Physical Component to the Mind

1. Elaine Schmidt, "Spacing Out after Staying Up Late? Here's Why," UCLA Newsroom, 2017, https://newsroom.ucla.edu/releases/spacing-out-after-staying-up-late.

2. Allison G. Harvey et al., "Overanxious and Underslept," *Nature Human Behaviour* 4 (2020): 100–110.

Chapter Ten Paying Attention to People

1. Holly Korbey, "The Power of Being Seen," Edutopia, 2017, https://www.edutopia.org/article/power-being-seen.

2. Chris Ewald, quoted in Korbey, "Power of Being Seen."

3. Elizabeth Allen et al., "Reasons for Divorce and Recollections of Premarital Intervention: Implications for Improving Relationship Education," *Couple Family Psychology* 2013 2(2): 131–45.

Chapter Eleven Stop, Pause, and Pay Attention—More on the Practice and Power of Paying Attention to People

1. Joan Kellerman, James Lewis, and James D. Laird, "Looking and Loving: The Effects of Mutual Gaze on Feelings of Romantic Love," *Journal of Research in Personality* 23, no. 2 (June 1989): 145–61.

2. Lydia Denworth, "How Eye Contact Prepares the Brain to Connect," *Psychology Today*, 2019, https://www.psychologytoday.com/us/blog/brain-waves /201902/how-eye-contact-prepares-the-brain-connect.

3. Brian Regan, "Me Monster," YouTube video, 4:24, posted by Steve Morgan, November 7, 2016, https://www.youtube.com/watch?v=2kLIe9vYop8&ab _channel=SteveMorgan.

4. Fred Rogers, *The World According to Mister Rogers* (New York: Hyperion, 2003), 175.

Chapter Twelve Entrepreneur Mindset Model

1. "What Happened to Scrub Daddy after Shark Tank?" SEOAves, 2022, https://seoaves.com/scrub-daddy-shark-tank-update/.

2. "About Us," Scrubdaddy.com, https://scrubdaddy.com/about/.

3. Ali Montag, "This $1 Billion Company Was Once Rejected on 'Shark Tank,'" CNBC, 2017, https://www.cnbc.com/2017/11/30/shark-tank-reject -doorbot-is-now-billion-dollar-company-ring.html.

Chapter Thirteen Farmer Mindset Model

1. Angone, *101 Secrets*, 54.

2. "The Biggest Little Farm," DocsforSchools, hotdocs.com, http://s3.amazon aws.com/assets.hotdocs.ca/doc/DFS19_BIGGEST-LITTLE-FARM.pdf.

3. Wendell Berry, Gary Snyder, and Chad Wriglesworth, eds., *Distant Neighbors* (Berkeley: Counterpoint, 2014).

4. Paul Kingsnorth, *The World-Ending Fire: The Essential Wendell Berry* (Berkeley: Counterpoint, 2019), reprint edition, 2.

Chapter Fourteen Writer Mindset Model

1. Samuel H. Scudder, "Agassiz and the Fish, by a Student," *American Poems*, 3rd ed. (Boston: Houghton, Osgood & Co., 1879), 450–54.

Chapter Sixteen Investigator Mindset Model

1. "Sherlock Holmes Awarded Title for Most Portrayed Literary Human Character in Film and TV," Guinness World Records News, May 14, 2012.

2. Arthur Conan Doyle, "A Scandal in Bohemia," in *The Adventures of Sherlock Holmes* (London: Strand Magazine, 1891), 62.

3. Dallas Willard, *Renovation of the Heart* (Colorado Springs: NavPress, 2002), 32.

Chapter Seventeen Monk Mindset Model

1. Angone, *25 Lies*, 179.
2. "The Conservation Legacy of Theodore Roosevelt," U.S. Department of the Interior, February 14, 2020, https://www.doi.gov/blog/conservation-legacy -theodore-roosevelt.
3. Theodore Roosevelt Timeline, National Park Service, https://www.nps .gov/thro/learn/historyculture/theodore-roosevelt-timeline.htm.
4. Roosevelt's diary entry for February, 14, 1884, quoted in Michelle Krowl, "New Online: Theodore Roosevelt Papers," October 17, 2018, Library of Congress Blog, https://blogs.loc.gov/loc/2018/10/new-online-theodore-roosevelt -papers/.

Conclusion A Life Lived Listening to Each Day

1. Doris Kearns Goodwin, *Team of Rivals: The Political Genius of Abraham Lincoln* (New York: Simon & Schuster, 2006), 17.
2. Abraham Lincoln, "Gettysburg Address," https://education.nationalgeo graphic.org/resource/gettysburg-address.
3. Alex Ayres, ed., *The Wit and Wisdom of Abraham Lincoln* (New York: Plume, 1995), 75.
4. Abraham Lincoln, "Remarks at the Monongahela House (February 14, 1861)," *The Collected Works of Abraham Lincoln*, ed. Roy P. Basler (New Brunswick, NJ: Rutgers University Press, 1953), 4:209.
5. Alexander K. McClure, *"Abe" Lincoln's Yarns and Stories* (New York: Western W. Wilson, 1901), Project Gutenberg, ebook, https://www.gutenberg.org /files/2517/2517-h/2517-h.htm.

JOIN PAUL ANGONE OVER AT
ALLGROANUP.COM

Your twenties and thirties are hard and important.
All Groan Up is a community dedicated to reminding
each one of us that we're not alone.

This *Groan*-Up life isn't simple or straightforward, and
we need a safe, real, hilarious space to talk about it.
Can't wait to see you there!

Connect with
BakerBooks
Relevant. Intelligent. Engaging.

Sign up for announcements about
new and upcoming titles at

BakerBooks.com/SignUp

@ReadBakerBooks